Cool Food

Cool Food

Books by Thomas Kostigen

NOVELS

Golden Dawn

Fatwa

NONFICTION

What Money Really Means

The Green Book

You Are Here

The Green Blue Book

The Big Handout

Extreme Weather Survival Guide

Hacking Planet Earth

Cool Food

KIDS

Extreme Weather

ROBERT DOWNEY JR.
& THOMAS KOSTIGEN

Cool Food

Erasing Your Carbon Footprint One Bite at a Time

BLACK STONE PUBLISHING

Cover design
Matthew Marley

Book design
Kathryn Galloway English

Illustrations of the authors
Nate Merritt

Recipe illustrations
Kathryn Galloway English
Matthew Marley

Recipe photographs
Raymond Craig
Amy Craig
Kathryn Galloway English
Finn English
Lysa Williams

First edition: 2024
ISBN 979-8-200-96237-2
Nature / Environmental Conservation & Protection

Version 1

Excerpt from *Sunlight and Seaweed: An Argument for How to
Feed, Power and Clean Up the World* by Tim Flannery
Copyright © 2017 Tim Flannery. Reprinted by permission of
Tim Flannery.

Some of the recipes that appear in this book have been
Americanized. See complete list of sources at CoolFoodBook.com.

Printed in the United States of America
Interior pages printed on certified paper

MIX
Paper | Supporting
responsible forestry
FSC® C008955

For Susan, Avri, Exton & Indio
—Robert Downey Jr.

For Jeannie & Junya
—Thomas Kostigen

Contents

Hi. Robert Downey here. Thank you for opening these pages and joining us on this little cool food adventure.

Cool food is a new category in the food space. It's a different way to eat to save the planet. It isn't a diet or a meal plan. It isn't even so much about food itself. Cool food is really about lifestyle—transformational shifts from little actions, experiences, and different choices. It's a holistic approach to making the world a whole lot better by simply making more informed decisions about something that each and every one of us does anyway—eat. If we wanted only to tell you which cool foods are best for the climate, we could have just sent you a list. This book is much more.

We look at food as the entry point for stories, like how my wife, Susan, and I fell in love in Montreal and the role maple syrup played in that. Or like the lightbulb moment I had over a meal in 2019 to start FootPrint Coalition, the company I founded to discover, partner, and invest in climate technologies.

Of course, the stories we tell in this book are unique. There are commentaries, anecdotes, factoids, and hard science that add up to something we think is worth your time to read from beginning to end. That said, you should be able to pick up the book anywhere in the following pages and get something out of it, whether it's a type of food you've never heard of, or an action you never thought about, or a new recipe. We're offering you a proverbial—and in some cases a literal—menu to think about, research more, or talk about with other people.

You'll see that the first part of the book is devoted to specific foods that are better for the planet than others. The second part of the book is about our relationship with food: where and how we buy it, and what we can do not to waste it. On that practical note, how we tell these stories and how they appear on the page should produce a different kind of reader experience for you as well—a fun and positive one.

So, you might ask, how did this journey begin? How did you, Downey, get on this cool food train? Well, Tom and I were already developing a television show together, so a book made a lot of sense to expand upon what we were doing and the stories we wanted to tell. The more positive impact we can make with our particular brand of storytelling, the better.

And with that, I'll turn it over to Kostigen.

I'll be brief:

I also wanted to give a quick note on how this book began . . . just in a bit more detail.

I was in London at Waterstones bookstore in Piccadilly, where I had stopped in, as I tend to do at any bookstore, to ask about what's selling and to see if I might sign copies of my books on the shelf. (Stores can't return signed books to publishers, so it's a bit of a sneaky author trick.) I asked where the climate books were, and the clerk said, "Oh, the bummer section? It's over there." Noted.

I happened to be on my way to a "Climavore" dinner event, where they served climate-friendly foods and gave

THOMAS

climate talks between courses. On the way to Hyde Park, I called Downey in Los Angeles, and I told him where I was headed. I also mentioned what the clerk had said.

"We need to do a food book and make it fun," he said right away.

Ting-a-ling.

I have worked in the climate space for more than two decades and have written more books than I have fingers. With Robert, though, my way of thinking about climate change, as well as how I was used to telling a story, had to change. We had to explore this topic together and express it in words as a team. Which is why we crafted a voice that represents us both. We also decided to be clear within each page that we're learning along with you. As Robert said, cool food is a new area. No one is really an expert in the field . . . namely because it isn't exactly a specific field.

Cool food is a loosely defined term. At its essence, it's about choosing foods that have a low, or even negative, carbon footprint to keep pollution out of the air. The more demand we create for these foods—certain nuts, fruits, vegetables, grains, and such—the more of them that have to be grown. And that means more greenhouse gases stay trapped in the ground. That's important.

Greenhouse gases trap heat in Earth's atmosphere. They include carbon dioxide, methane, water vapor, ozone, and nitrous oxide, among others. For the purposes of this book, we concentrated mostly on carbon dioxide, or CO_2. It's the foremost greenhouse gas emitted by human activity.

Reducing our global carbon emissions is likely the biggest environmental challenge we face today. Emitting less carbon leads to lower temperature rise. We usually go about doing this through our energy use—using fewer fossil fuels that emit lots of carbon and replacing them with alternative sources that emit less. Think of cool foods as the equivalent of those alternative power sources— food's solar or wind power.

It should be noted that we did not take an exhaustive approach to examine each and every cool food out there. Quite the contrary. We chose those foods and the related food issues that we thought would make for good stories. And those stories are what follows.

Part One

What's Cool to Eat

ANCIENT GRAINS

Ancient foods, not old, and definitely not spoiled. Man, are they good.

To begin, we decided to go back in time and follow the path of food into the future. We learned that certain types of grains are better than others, and technology is helping to breed ancient grains in new ways, making them intentionally better for the planet and helping to cool temperatures. This dose of information surprised us. We suspected large perennial tree foods, such as fruits and nuts, would be mainstay cool foods—and they are. We didn't think we'd be discussing grains in this book in any positive sense. But it turns out that not all grains are alike.

From what we understand, it looks like it's going to take a double-barrel approach to make grains more sustainable: rekindling our relationships with ancient grains as well as engineering plants differently to capture and store more CO_2. Food scientists told us that they are breeding new kinds of perennial grains that can replace

FAST FACT: "Ancient grains" is actually a marketing term that attempts to describe grains that haven't been altered much over time by modern farming, which uses innovations to make grains grow better/faster or to breed new varieties.

WHAT'S OLD IS TRENDY AGAIN

A big study of food shoppers found that half are interested in ancient grains and nearly half already buy them. Black rice, quinoa, and chia top the list of what we choose most. And even though these grains aren't super terrific carbon storers, they do take less energy to produce than lots of other foods and are therefore "cooler."

rice, wheat, sorghum, legumes, oilseeds, and other types of common grains. This is a big breakthrough in the effort to help roll back the negative effects of climate change.

Grains are a huge component of our current diets. Rice, corn, and wheat make up the majority of what we and the rest of the global population eat. And so, these are also the top grains grown. They are largely harvested seasonally and therefore are relatively

Cereal Grains

The grains most familiar to us are part of the grass family. A grass that is grown to be eaten as food is called a cereal.

COMMON CEREAL GRAINS:

WHEAT | CORN | RICE | BARLEY | OATS | RYE | SORGHUM

From these we make bread, pasta, cakes, cookies, breakfast cereals—even popcorn.

Our Limited Options

There used to be many different types of plants from which to feed people. However, in the past century, as farmers began to refine their crops to those that were higher yielding, about 75 percent of the world's plant genetic diversity has been erased. Now, most of our food supply is from only twelve plants and five animal species:

PLANTS	ANIMALS
1. Wheat	1. Chicken
2. Rice	2. Pig
3. Corn	3. Cow
4. Sugarcane	4. Buffalo
5. Soy	5. Goat
6. Potatoes	
7. Cassava	
8. Palm	
9. Millet	
10. Sorghum	
11. Groundnuts	
12. Sweet potatoes	

poor carbon capturers; plants aren't left in the ground to act as carbon sinks. They are torn up, and with them goes a lot of the carbon they stored. That means they aren't significantly helping the climate-change problem we are facing. In fact, seasonal harvesting can make the climate problem far worse.

So, what if seasonal crop foods were made into perennials? It turns out, that would be a boon for the planet. We read an interesting piece by columnist Tamar Haspel in the *Washington Post* that explained how and why perennial grains are growing

WHY SEASONAL CROPS AREN'T COOL

When a seasonal crop is harvested, it loses all of its carbon intake and depletes the soil of 40 percent of its carbon content. All that carbon is released into the air, adding significantly to climate change.

in popularity: "Carbon loss dates back to the first time a farmer ever turned over virgin soil, but it's only in the past couple of decades that momentum has built among farmers and researchers trying to reverse things. There's a major obstacle, though: 400 million (ish) acres of annuals, crops that have to be planted anew every year. While annuals are very good at growing seeds (usually the plant part we eat), they're not so good at locking carbon in the soil. In fact, they're pretty bad at it."

The *Post* also reported that the Land Institute, a nonprofit organization based

Annual, Biennial, Perennial

Different plants have different life spans. The longer a plant or tree lives, the more opportunity it has to capture and store carbon dioxide, keeping the heat-trapping substance from the air, where it would raise temperatures. Annual plants grow and die in a year. Biennial plants have a two-year life cycle. But perennial plants and trees live for many years.

Cool Food: KERNZA

Kernza is an ancient grain from Eurasia that has been planted and grown in the US, but typically only on a small scale for livestock. It has big roots—up to ten feet long—and big potential for climate change. It captures significant amounts of carbon from the air and keeps it stored in the ground.

in Kansas dedicated to revamping the agricultural food system to make it more sustainable, has embarked on a number of programs to replace annual food crops with perennial food crops at scale.

Its big bet is on Kernza. When we spoke with the Land Institute, they told us that Kernza can be used in baked goods, beer, and cereal, or be cooked like rice or barley. You can find Kernza at some stores and served at some restaurants. Easier still, you can order it online.

Just after the July Fourth holiday, Rachel Stroer, president of the Land Institute, agreed to speak with us and fill us in on the perennial grain story and a whole lot more. Standing outside her home in Texas under the shady trees of her backyard, she captured the topic perfectly.

"Our natural ecosystems are very different from our agricultural systems in two key ways: natural ecosystems feature almost exclusively perennial plants, and they grow in diverse mixtures. Diverse perennial ecosystems are what build the soils upon which we eat today. And none of our agriculture—our grain agriculture in particular—systems have either of those features. Our grain ag systems are almost exclusively annual crops grown

MONOCULTURE VS. POLYCULTURE

Monoculture farming is when a single crop is planted and grown on the same land, whereas polyculture farming means growing different crops on the same land by either rotating them or growing them next to one another. Polyculture builds healthier soil because it's adding a variety of nutrients to the soil from the different crops grown.

in monoculture systems. So, they die or are killed every year. They can't produce grain over and over again. And it is that disturbance of the soil that is really the source of most of the problems in our agriculture system. It's why we put toxic chemicals on them. It's why we're constantly trying to replace the ecological function that plants are accustomed to living in and thriving in and instead destroying soil with chemical, man-made processes or inputs. So, what the Land Institute has been working on over the last twenty or thirty years is developing a diverse perennial grain agriculture. That means starting at square one to develop new, novel perennial grain crops," Stroer explained.

In other words, we could replace almost all the world's wheat crops, for instance, with a new variety—Kernza wheat—that is better for the soil and captures carbon at a magnificent rate and stores it, helping to mitigate climate change while at the same time feeding the world.

Wheat is the most grown and consumed food in the world and takes up more land area than any other food crop. Replacing it is a tall order. A lot of growth and a lot of replacement crops would have to go into the ground. Still, even on a small scale, every bit helps the planet. There are no significant perennial grain crops out in the world.

"I think of our work as transformational. There are 1.1 billion hectares of grain production in the world. Almost all of those are annual monocultures. Our goal over time is to transition a majority of those acres, or hectares, into perennial polycultures. We have to develop those crops, and then we have to develop the diverse systems to

FAST FACT:
Our annual grain crops have been in development for ten thousand years or more.

8

THE MOST ANCIENT GRAIN

The most ancient grain is einkorn wheat. It dates back centuries and is believed to be the first cultivated crop in the Tigris-Euphrates region, where farming began. Einkorn was reportedly first grown specifically for human consumption in the mountains of southeastern Turkey. It then made its way around the Middle East and Europe. In fact, according to Einkorn.com (which provides all you need to know and more about this type of wheat), Europe's oldest mummy, Ötzi the Iceman, was found to have ground-up einkorn wheat in his stomach, likely from bread.

Einkorn is a simple grain and doesn't contain the D chromosome that is connected to wheat intolerance. Modern wheat has forty-two chromosomes, whereas einkorn only has fourteen. It also contains more protein and antioxidants than modern wheat, which is why it's deemed a "superfood." It's now mostly grown in Morocco, France, Turkey, and eastern Europe.

But is einkorn a cool food? Its wild form and ability to diversify agricultural land help keep soil healthy. Production is light on energy, too. Overall, wheat—not just einkorn—has a low carbon footprint (about half that of rice, for example). And einkorn has a longer root system than modern wheat, making it capable of shuttling more carbon deeper into the ground. While its Kernza cousin in the wheatgrass family takes the top spot as a cool food, einkorn is a good option.

grow them in. We have to train the farmers how to grow them and hear from chefs about totally new inputs to the culinary experience. And they have to say, 'Oh, does it work? Does it make for a better beer? Does it rise? Can it be a sourdough?' It's going to take all those things falling in place. It's going to take decades of work.

"So, I think that the thing that a consumer can do right now—besides buying Kernza or some of the few perennial grains out there right now—is to really understand the devastation and extractive nature of

Methane:

Methane as a greenhouse gas is even worse for the climate than carbon dioxide. It has twenty-five times the warming power of CO_2 and is responsible for about a third of global temperature rise.

Grain Energy

In general, producing about two pounds of wheat takes about a kilogram of energy. How much energy is that, and how does that compare to other common grain crops? Let's take a look at some rough comparisons.

The energy needed to produce 2 pounds of ...	is roughly equivalent to driving a car ...
OATS	0.75 miles
SORGHUM	0.75 miles
CORN	1.5 miles
WHEAT	2.5 miles
RYE	2.5 miles
RICE	5–6 miles*

(*depending on the variety)

our current annual grain agro-ecosystem. I mean, it's vast. It's on different continents. Seventy percent of our ag lands in the world are in grain production. A huge portion of the soil that we depend on to sustain human life is in grains. And I think a lot of times we like to imagine, especially progressive and privileged people like myself, that if all the world ate at the farmers' market we would be okay. I'm not anti–farmer's market at all, but that's not enough," said Stroer.

FAST FACT:
The global production of rice has about the same climate footprint as the aviation industry. That's huge!

Her urge? "Eat more perennials," she said. "And I would say there's also an opportunity to advocate for perennials in policy. We spend billions of dollars on incremental improvements to annual grain crops, much of which goes to feed cows. We're spending billions of dollars to feed this animal protein, and if

"I was in the middle of filming *Oppenheimer* in New Mexico when I came to appreciate Native American cuisine. When you taste the food, you feel the respect for the ingredients and their preparation. There are a ton of Native American restaurants in New Mexico, curiously, something you don't find in other states—even in California, where I live; trust me, I've looked and tried ordering on Uber Eats . . . but I digress . . . Preparing ancient grains according to their natural conditions seems like a no-brainer to get us to a better climate."

Cool Food: AMARANTH

Amaranth is tasty as porridge. It's prepared pretty much the same way you might make your hot cereal with oats: add water, milk, or your favorite plant-based substitute, and serve. Add some cool fruit, nuts, or berries for a truly earth-friendly meal.

just a fraction of those billions could be converted, it could start the possibility of a perennial future. Then we might have a chance of sustaining ourselves for the next ten thousand years on this planet without killing a bunch of other animals and species in the process."

Perhaps including ourselves.

Many farmers say they have come to realize that soil is being ruined by, among other things, monoculture farming practices that reduce crop yields by half and, if left unabated, could destroy 90 percent of Earth's healthy soil by 2050. Which is why there is now a big push to bring ancient grains and growing practices back to help revive the soil and reintroduce

many historic crops into our food system.

Half the world's population eats rice every day, and the amount of rice grown and land that it occupies is staggering, as is the impact on the climate. More than seven hundred million tons of rice are grown annually on about 160 million hectares. (There are about 2.5 acres per hectare.) That's

FAST FACT:
PR23 is a newly developed form of perennial rice with deeper root systems, which ostensibly allow more carbon to be stored and help to improve soil structure.

about three times the size of Spain!

Rice accounts for 2.5 percent of all greenhouse gas emissions that we produce and 12 percent of all methane emissions. The reason that rice produces so much methane has to do with the way it grows. Rice grows on paddies, or flooded fields. The water stops oxygen—and CO_2 for that matter—from reaching the ground. And the bacteria that grow in the water emit methane.

Researchers say that dry, arable land typically stores about three and a half tons of carbon dioxide per year per acre. Which means dry grains like wheat really should be our go-to cereals. Still, not all rice grows on lowland paddies. Upland, or dryland, rice is also out there for the taking. That's the cool food choice to make for rice. A couple of common upland rice varieties are titian rose and hayayuki, and sometimes the package label will say how the rice was grown.

Another way we can help is by seeking out old grains like amaranth, which is similar to quinoa; American persimmons, which are similar to plums; ayocotes, which are like black beans; dulse, which is seaweed; and blue camas, which is similar to parsnips. These are just some of the foods that we learned were regularly eaten by Native Americans that could be brought back to popularity, bringing about a more diverse food menu for us eaters and terra firma alike.

Gluten-Free

Gluten is a protein found in wheat and other grains such as rye. It's a naturally occurring substance, and most people digest it just fine. But some people have reactions to gluten that make them feel sick. Celiac disease and gluten intolerance cause gastrointestinal issues. Which is why you'll often see products that are labeled "gluten-free."

Whole Grains:

Whole grains contain all three parts of their kernels—the bran (outer skin), endosperm (the biggest part of the starchy center), and germ (the embryo part that can sprout into a new plant). Refining grains removes the embryo and bran and leaves them with about 25 percent less protein and fewer nutrients. Which is why whole grains are considered healthier.

According to the WHOLE GRAINS COUNCIL, there are twenty-two common whole grains:

- amaranth
- barley
- buckwheat
- bulgur
- corn
- einkorn
- farro / emmer
- fonio
- freekeh
- Kamut® Khorasan
- kañiwa
- millet
- oats
- quinoa
- rice
- rye
- sorghum / milo
- spelt
- teff
- triticale
- wheat
- wild rice

Yet, as we've discussed, the carbon storage capacity of the lot varies greatly. Compared to meat, grains are climate positive. But individually, the Whole Grains Council highlighted Kernza as one of our best climate-fixing foods.

There are also new grains on the horizon. Food scientists tell us that they have figured out ways to develop cooler grains through genetic manipulation. One way is to reengineer plants' roots so they are larger and longer. That keeps more CO_2 in the ground even if the plant itself dies. When plants die, much of the carbon they've stored goes back into the air and adds to a warming atmosphere. The other way is to make plants more drought resistant. This allows them to live longer and, in turn, keep more carbon out of the air. Such advancements are out of our hands, directly. But what we can do is choose foods that historically are more drought tolerant. According to the Whole Grains Council, which undertook an investigation into the matter of sustainable grains and whose findings we eagerly followed, "ancient" and heirloom grains are the best place for sustainable food. The council said:

Einkorn is the most drought-tolerant of wheat varieties, though spelt and emmer both perform well too. Teff (a type of millet) and sorghum, two grains native to Africa, both thrive in drought, and teff is adaptable to waterlogged soils as well. Proso millet, the most commonly grown millet in the US, is generally recognized as having the lowest water requirement of any grain crop, and pearl millet, commonly grown in Africa and Asia, is the most tolerant of extremes of heat and drought.

In addition to encouraging different varieties of grains, a lot can be accomplished by crossbreeding grains from different parts of the world. A group called Protein2Food is doing this in Denmark. It's developing proteins from ancient grains that can be bred wisely through better crop management and then massively adopted. The goal is to enhance protein production from plants by 25

Cool Food: MILLET

Drought-tolerant grains such as millets can live longer in more extreme weather conditions, and that means their plants have more staying power to capture carbon dioxide and help cool the climate. When plants die, their carbon-storing potential disappears, and the carbon they consumed over their lives is released back into the atmosphere. The best of these drought-tolerant breeds is pearl millet, which is common in Asia and Africa. In the US, look for proso millet.

percent. One of its big success stories is South American quinoa that was bred with different varieties to make it more climate resilient to grow in Scandinavia. The "new" ancient grain now sells in more than seventy countries.

Supply and variety need to escalate and expand for us to have more choices. This is what the Whole Grains Council is set up to do. It's promoting education and growing programs to put more sustainable grains on store shelves.

"There's a whole-grain revival," said Caroline Sluyter, the program director for the Whole Grains Council. She explained that the council looks to promote more "traditional foodways"—foods and culinary practices that have been passed on for generations without corruption by modern processing methods.

"One of the things that happens when you refine a grain is you're stripping away the bran and the germ, which actually are the most flavorful parts of the kernel. The interesting thing about whole grains is that each variety of grain has its own characteristic taste. Some are nutty. Some are peppery. Some are buttery. I think of kino wheat, which is just so buttery without doing anything to it.

Some of them are kind of sweet. They have tons of notes of butterscotch and interesting things like that. You get some that are chewy. I think of wheat berries that kind of pop in your teeth. You can get really sticky consistencies with oatmeal or polenta. Some can be cooked to be light and fluffy, like millet. And then you can also have these smooth porridge-like textures with grains like amaranth and teff, where if you're adding that to a soup, it's going to make it kind of silky and smooth," she said.

Sluyter said there's been a significant uptick in interest in whole grains of late, especially among younger consumers, because of increased awareness of their health and eco benefits. Whole grains have been found to help prevent cardiovascular disease, type 2 diabetes, certain types of cancers, and inflammation, she says. They can also help people maintain a healthy body weight. "So there's a really wide variety of benefits that have been shown to be kind of particular to whole

grains and not true of refined grains in the same way."

Whole grains check a lot of boxes when it comes to sustainability, too. "Number one is that they are considered by some to be the most important source of food worldwide. They provide about 50 percent of the calories that humans consume. And then on the other side, they also are some of the least intensive foods to produce. They require much less water than even fruits and vegetables. They're easier to store. They're easier to transport. They just make a lot of sense from a sustainable perspective," she said.

Moreover, many are better adapted to changing climate conditions. "You can look at ancient wheats like einkorn and emmer, which do much better in drought conditions than other kinds of more common, modern wheat varieties. Look at different types of millet like teff and grains like sorghum. These are grains that thrive in drought conditions. Teff is also adaptable to waterlogged soils, which is kind of neat. And millets in general just stand up well to extreme heat and drought conditions. It's so important to find crops like that and to move consumer consumption habits in that direction because we're already seeing the impacts on wheat, corn, and rice production due to rising temperatures. I think we can expect lower yields in the coming years," Sluyter said.

To help us shoppers better identify which products are made with whole grains, the Whole Grains Council developed a certification label, the Whole Grain stamp. "This provides consumers with another tool to help them identify and find whole-grain products when they're shopping. The nutrition facts panel and the ingredients label on many products don't always make clear whether that product contains whole grains and how much whole grain is in it, which are two things that our stamp does," Sluyter explained.

Look for it.

▲ ▲ ▲ ▲ ▲ ▲ ▲ ▲ ▲

There are many different varieties of grains and by-products of grains. Some grains are actually cereals, and some seeds are called grains, too. So, the grain world, we found, is pretty complex. The simple fact is that over time we have winnowed our food group too much. Our new narrow offering of relatively few foods that feed the planet is depleting plants' and the ground's abilities to offset climate change. Broadening our food choices, especially among the most basic foods that we eat—grains—can turn climate change and a lot of the planet's problems around.

Having more food choices closer to home is yet another strategy for us to consider when it comes to enhancing our selection of cool foods.

18

What You Can Do Today

- Go for ancient or whole grains at the store.

- Upland, dry rice is a good option. Look for titian rose and hayayuki.

- Remember wheat is the best cool food to eat.

- When it comes to wheat, try to find Kernza. Einkorn is a good second choice.

- Drought-tolerant grains such as millet are also good choices. Look for proso millet in the US.

- Amaranth, American persimmon, ayocote, and blue camas were common Native American foods that we could stand to revive. They're good for the soil and help to keep the ground "cool."

NOTE: You can make this recipe without presoaking the millet, but the texture will be coarser and you may need to add additional almond milk to loosen the grain. Also plan to add approximately 5 minutes of cooking time to the millet before adding the banana and other ingredients.

Recipe courtesy of Oldways Cultural Food Traditions

Banana Millet Breakfast Porridge

INGREDIENTS

½ c. **MILLET,** presoaked overnight

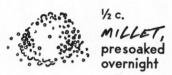

½ tbsp. **GROUND CINNAMON**

1 large ripe **BANANA**

1 tbsp. **ALMOND BUTTER** or nut butter of choice

½ c. **ALMOND MILK** or other milk of choice

1 tsp. **HONEY** (optional)

METHOD

1 Drain the millet and add it to a medium saucepan. Toast the millet over low to medium heat, until it is slightly browned and gives off a nutty aroma, about 3 to 5 minutes. Be careful not to burn the millet.

2 Add 2 cups of water and cinnamon to the saucepan with the millet. Raise the heat to medium-high so that the water will start to boil.

3 Once the water is boiling, turn the heat down to low and cover. Let the millet simmer for approximately 20 minutes, or until it becomes creamy and the water has been absorbed. Remove from the heat and leave the cover on.

4 Mash the banana with a fork and add to the millet.

5 In a small bowl, whisk the almond milk and almond butter together, and add to the millet, stirring to incorporate. Taste, and add the honey if desired. Return the millet to low heat for 2 to 3 minutes until warmed through.

6 Serve as is, or add extra almond milk, sliced bananas, or nuts as garnish.

21

Recipe developed by Beth Dooley @ BethDooleysKitchen.com

Kernza Vanilla Butter Cake

INGREDIENTS

1 c.
MAPLE SUGAR or **LIGHT BROWN SUGAR**

3 **LARGE EGGS**, lightly beaten

1 tsp. **VANILLA**

1 stick (½ c.) **UNSALTED BUTTER** melted

1 tsp. **SALT**

1 c. **KERNZA FLOUR**

METHOD

1 Preheat the oven to 350°F.

2 Grease and lightly flour a 6-cup Bundt pan or 8½-inch loaf pan.

3 In a large bowl, beat together the sugar, eggs, vanilla, and salt.

4 Slowly whisk in half of the melted butter until well combined. Stir in ½ cup of the flour until well combined. Then mix in the remaining butter and then the flour. Stir until the batter is even with no lumps.

5 Turn the batter into the pan and bake until a toothpick inserted in the middle comes out clean, about 25 to 35 minutes.

6 Cool on a wire rack for about 15 minutes; gently turn the pan over and tap until the cake slides out.

FRUITS

It's time to get exotic,
and maybe get to know jack.

Moving up in size and matter from grains, we turned to fruits and vegetables. With a toss of the coin, we decided to focus on fruits first.

Fruits and vegetables often get grouped into the same basket, but there's a technical difference: Fruits have seeds and grow from a plant's flower. Vegetables, on the other hand, are composed of roots, stems, and leaves. To a large degree, taste is what distinguishes a fruit from a vegetable. Fruits are usually sweet-tasting or tart-flavored—the kind of thing we'd have for dessert.

When it comes to fruits, one of the most carbon-capturing kinds that you can eat is citrus fruit. But it gets complicated. Fertilizers, preservatives, refrigeration, and waste are important factors that can add enormously to a fruit's carbon footprint. And that is the case with citrus.

Citrus fruits are among the most widely grown and traded types of fruit in the world. Common citrus are

FAST FACT:
Every acre of apple orchard can absorb as much as twenty tons of CO_2 a year—the same amount of pollution created by burning 2,250 gallons of gas.

THE DAWN OF APPLES

Apple trees are native to Kazakhstan, where the oldest apple tree in the world still exists. The *Malus sieversii* (wild apple) is the mother of the domestic apple and tastes most similar to Golden Delicious apples. Apparently if it wasn't for birds and bears, the modern apple may never have made it onto Thanksgiving tables or teachers' desks. Animals allegedly carried apple seeds out of Kazakhstan and into the Middle East, where Romans fancied the fruit. They began trading them, and soon seeds were being planted around the world.

Apples have done the world a lot of good keeping carbon at bay, even if apple trees push more of the carbon they store into the fruit they bear. Other fruits store more carbon in their trunks, roots, and leaves. Still, on a net basis, apple trees are positive for the climate.

oranges, lemons, limes, and grapefruits, with dozens of hybrids like limequat and citrange. Oranges are by far the most grown fruit among those that are sold. And their orchards store more carbon per hectare than any other kind of naturally grown, land-based food except nuts. However, oranges are often processed into juice, which in many cases negates much of the good carbon capturing they can do for the planet. We found that water, energy use, additives, transportation, storage, and other necessities add up to big drains on natural resources.

That led us to one of the next best fruits for the planet: the apple. Apples, of course, are grown in orchards. They are harvested all over the world, and they are increasingly getting a lot of love for their climate-fixing potential.

While organic apples and oranges may be among the best cool fruits that you can swallow, olives, even though they are more tart than sweet, are right up there. As a raw food item, olives have roughly half the carbon footprint of an apple, and they can keep for long periods, meaning they don't need as much energy for temperature-controlled warehousing, which adds to any product's carbon footprint. Just mind your use of olive oil. Similar to how the process of juicing fruits increases their carbon footprints, so too does the process of grinding olives and extracting their oil.

In our research, our original idea was to exclude water, transportation, as well as any other externalities and pretend that we are living in the wild, foraging around and gathering our food the old-fashioned way. That would allow us to see very simply which foods from which plants store the most carbon, allowing us to compare, proverbially, apples to apples.

FAST FACT:
Dates are among the best fruit you can eat for the climate, with half the carbon footprint of even an apple.

HOW MUCH FRUIT SHOULD YOU EAT?

Fruit should be 40 percent of a person's daily diet, but 90 percent of the US population doesn't eat enough. That's a big gap. Filling it can make the planet a cooler place.

The reality is modern farming brings with it a lot of pollution. Analysts who assign carbon footprints to foods say growing methods, storage, and transportation must be taken into account to make a fair assessment of how much energy and, in turn, pollution come from a food getting to market.

Take bananas, for example. If they aren't organic, they tend to require more agrochemicals to grow than any other crop in the world, analysts say.

Banana plantations are associated with monocropping, which causes the "soil structure and quality to be so poor farmers must use chemical fertilizers to encourage plant growth and fruit production," the ethical consumer guide HEALabel explains. "Pesticides and fertilizers contaminate ground water and become airborne, creating pollution, [but] monocropping is not an issue if the product is organic," HEALabel claims.

....

WHERE SHOULD YOUR BANANAS COME FROM?

While bananas for us are largely associated with Central and South America—Ecuador being the largest grower there—India is the world's biggest producer of bananas. We also learned that some grow in the US, in Florida and Hawaii. To save the carbon emissions from shipping, go for organic bananas that were grown closest to where you live.

So, as such, bananas as a group are only rated moderately sustainable.

This is where it all gets a bit messy. You have the size of a tree, the health of a tree, the soil quality from which a tree grows, never mind how the fruit is picked—by someone with a machete or by a fossil-fuel-powered tractor pluming all sorts of greenhouse gases into the air. Whether or not the picked fruit has to be stored at a particular temperature and how far it must travel by truck, plane, or ship to make it onto a grocery store shelf—these factors make a difference in how much or how little carbon is stored on a net basis. Yet naturally, banana trees do trap their fair share of carbon pollution. If we were to just pick a banana off a tree in the wild, there wouldn't be any associated pollution. Alas, those opportunities are rare.

Then there's how the fruit is stored. Food companies told us that they have storage facilities that regulate the ethylene gas that is naturally produced

28

by certain fruits, causing them to ripen. Slowing the release of this gas allows the fruits to remain "fresh" longer and not spoil. You can do this at home by keeping your fruits separated and in different bins. Food researchers say that by regulating the ethylene gas of foods that are grown overseas and imported, we can have lower carbon footprints because shipping produces less pollution than the energy used for

STORAGE-FRIENDLY FRUITS

Tomatoes, along with bananas, pears, and apples can all be picked and stored before they are ripe. This adds to their coolness because they can be stored for long periods, meaning we can stock up.

"'What's my favorite fruit?' Good question. There's a scene in *The Avengers* where I offer Chris Evans and Mark Ruffalo blueberries. It's gotten a fair bit of attention because it wasn't in the script. I was just hungry, and offering them blueberries seemed like the human thing to do. Food does that; it's a great equalizer. I think we can all agree that eating in a more thoughtful and global way is the right path forward. Now that I know strawberries aren't actually berries but fruit that can do a whole lotta good, I wish I would've had strawberries on set that day."

FRESH, FROZEN, OR CANNED?

When it comes to fresh versus frozen versus canned, it can be a toss-up of which is more climate friendly given the considerations of the season, transportation, refrigeration, waste, packaging, preparation, and processing. The safest bet, if you're uncertain, is to go for what's frozen because it avoids waste, and growing seasons are less of a factor. (Note that fresh and local is in theory the best cool food choice if all portions are consumed and there is no spoilage; tall orders!)

more production. Preventing spoilage saves more carbon emissions than growing more supply. This is a really important and underreported point.

Another common fruit that is tough to pin down but has a low carbon footprint is the strawberry. Strawberries, which are not berries and are technically a multi-fruit, grow in all sorts of weather conditions and are great climate fighters on their own.

But overall, berries aren't big carbon sequesters because they mostly grow on small plants that aren't big enough to store lots of carbon dioxide. In fact, the carbon footprint difference between berry plants is marginal. The website MyEmissions.green, which provides a free carbon calculator of foods, shows the same low carbon rating (which means good) for berries as a group.

That doesn't mean all berries are grown alike. Some edible berries are grown on larger trees—mulberries, Canadian buffaloberries, rowan, elderberries, and certain hackberries, to name several. These have more carbon-storing power. So, berries are fine choices, and healthy ones too, even if they don't generally pack a lot of carbon-fixing power.

Strawberries, bananas, and most fruits we find on display at the grocery store likely aren't going to fix the climate. But there is one lesser-known fruit that just might: jackfruit. Some environmentalists say that it could save the world.

Jackfruit looks like a giant—and we mean giant, they can weigh over one hundred pounds—pear with the mumps. They are super nutritious and versatile. Their meat is often used as a substitute for pulled pork, taco meat, cheesesteaks, and even crab cakes. (We've found it particularly good in tacos.)

Jackfruit trees are relatively easy to grow and have been thriving in Florida for decades. Although

The Top Ten Fruits in the US

The fruits that we grow most in the United States in order of quantity are:

1. Grapes
2. Apples
3. Oranges
4. Strawberries
5. Lemons
6. Tangerines and mandarins
7. Pears
8. Peaches
9. Grapefruits
10. Cranberries

These are all terrific choices to help keep more carbon out of the atmosphere and to help keep us healthy.

See **CHAPTER SEVEN** for some tips on when specific cool foods are in season.

Cool Food: *MANGOES*

Mangoes are one of the best foods for the environment. They have a super low carbon footprint and are full of health benefits. In America, though, mangoes don't even make the top ten list of most popular fruits. Perhaps we can stand to eat more.

they're indigenous to India, the climate conditions are similar, and jackfruit trees adapted well. (It's when trees from different climates are maladaptive to where they are grown that they require more care in the form of fertilizers and pesticides that can harm the soil and the climate.) Jackfruit trees store vast amounts of carbon because of their size and resiliency. They can also adapt well to different environments. And, as mentioned, the meat of the fruit is versatile. Jackfruit have about the same small carbon footprint as lentils (a cool food we'll talk about in the next chapter). They just need to catch on.

Abiu, bael, jujube, loquat, and lychee are also climate-positive fruits and could have big potential with wider acceptance. Never heard of them? Neither had we. But they are grown in abundance on other continents, and planting more of them could make for a big climate win.

While exotic and lesser-known fruits can and should be produced on a bigger scale, we are told the fruits we are used to eating can and should be brought to market differently, taking into account growing seasons, as well as where they are grown.

Tomatoes are the most consumed fruit in the world and are a relatively good cool food choice, and so we were surprised to learn that if you live in Boston, where the weather gets nippy for a good portion of the year, then locally grown tomatoes may not be the best option; a tomato from South America might be. Depending on the time of year, tomatoes may need the comforts of a greenhouse, which requires energy. The energy for that heat also produces carbon emissions, and that can add significantly to the carbon footprint of the tomatoes grown in these "hothouse" conditions.

"Follow the seasons," Luis Acuña told us. And as the president and CEO of Viva Tierra Organic, an organic fruit farming operation in Washington State, he knows what he's talking about. Just in from the field, Luis spoke to us early one summer morning, when temperatures had soared to record highs, scorching the land and damaging crops and, in turn, crimping yields.

"Many retailers don't care to let people know if the fruit that they're eating today was picked in the last few hours or a year ago. You won't know until you bring it home and then the fruit is milly or all wrinkled and dehydrated and with hardly any flavor. But it's still organic," he said. "Larger-scale production, they're in the market with fruit year-round."

That's why the certified organic label alone isn't a good barometer of taste and freshness. Understanding where something is grown, and when, matters most. Even if that fruit is grown half a world away.

"I think a lot of people don't realize that if you buy fruit off-season that it's probably not better for the planet, even if it's from a local farm, because you're eating food that has been grown in a greenhouse or hothouse with fertilizers and other things that would need to be done with certain types of produce in order to make that feasible to grow in the wintertime versus importing something via ship because there, you know, the carbon emissions associated with the ship are very low. And you're just getting a fresher fruit and you're also supporting a local community somewhere else with fewer emissions. So I think that's something that's important to underscore," he said.

To be sure, the organic label matters. It means consideration has been given to chemicals and the like in the growing process. And organically grown fruit can help the soil, and that can help the climate. But Acuña said we should continue to think globally when it comes to the climate, and that sometimes means eating globally, too. It's the types of farmers—small-scale, organic, no matter where they are—who are practicing more wholesome methods who are key to the climate solution, he said.

"For a while we were on this globalization trend, and now we're not. Now countries have pulled back, and we have all these supply chain issues after the pandemic. And it's getting more challenging, to be honest with you—more expensive. If this trend doesn't get reversed, we're going to have a lot of farmers go out of business,

especially the smaller farmers, whether they are domestic or from abroad.

"We represent many farmers in the state of Washington. But then during the import season [winter], we represent growers from Argentina and Chile as well. For instance, we are right now [summer] in the middle of our California season, shipping Bartlett pears from the Sacramento Delta region. We just get to market right away, no matter from where. The logistics are quite simple here with domestic and local supply. And then from overseas, we partnered up with growers so they can book shipments of large quantities of fruit. They come either to the West Coast or the East Coast, and then from there most routes go straight to the stores. So there's the way to have the freshest product on the shelves at all times," Acuña said.

The difficulty lies in consumer awareness. The easiest way to get educated, Acuña said, is to rely on what tastes good and fresh. That should lead

34

How to Read PLU Codes

The price lookup code (PLU) on a sticker attached to a fruit or vegetable lets you know if it's grown organically.

Four digits:	The produce has been conventionally grown.	
Five digits, beginning with 9:	The produce has been grown organically.	
Five digits, beginning with 8:	The produce has been genetically modified.	

The pesticides and fertilizers used in conventional farming methods can add significantly to a food's carbon footprint. So look for barcode stickers with five digits and the number 9 to do what's best for Planet Earth.

you to the attributes of what made the fruit taste that way. Then it's time to speak up to retailers about freshness, or quality, as well as about organics. Growers can create supply, but it's on us consumers to bring about demand.

Now that we've covered some of the sweet stuff fruit has to offer, let's get a taste of the role veggies can play in keeping things cool.

What You Can Do Today

- **Know the season of where a fruit is grown and use that as your fresh fruit purchase guide.**

- **Pick fruits that come from bigger trees, which store more carbon.**

- **Try something exotic, like mangoes or jackfruit.**

- **Choose organic produce when possible. Look for a 9 on price codes that have five digits next to the barcode on a product label to know it's organic.**

- **Eat dates; they are among the best fruits for the climate.**

- **Fresh, frozen, and canned fruit overall have relatively the same carbon footprint. But the safest bet for cool fruit is to buy frozen.**

Recipe courtesy of Vegetarian Society

Pineapple Stuffed with Mixed Jerk Vegetables

INGREDIENTS

For the Jerk:

2 LARGE ONIONS, peeled and finely chopped

1 tbsp. RAW SUGAR

4 cloves GARLIC, crushed

1 tbsp. TAMARI

1 SCOTCH BONNET or HABAÑERO CHILI, deseeded and finely chopped

2 tsp. ground ALLSPICE

1-inch piece ROOT GINGER, peeled and grated

1 tsp. GROUND CINNAMON

2 tbsp. LEMON JUICE

1 tsp. DRIED THYME

SALT

2 tbsp. OLIVE OIL

freshly ground BLACK PEPPER

For the Chopped Vegetables:

2 small EGGPLANTS, cut into chunks

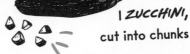

1 ZUCCHINI, cut into chunks

½ SWEET POTATO, very thinly sliced

1 PLANTAIN (or 2 GREEN BANANAS), diced (you can find plantains at Latin American markets)

10 OKRA pods, finely sliced

37

3 **SWEET BABY ORANGE PEPPERS**
and
3 **SWEET BABY RED PEPPERS,**
deseeded and sliced into rings

2 tbsp. **CILANTRO,** chopped

1 (14-oz.) can **PETITE DICED TOMATOES**

1 **SCOTCH BONNET** or **HABAÑERO CHILI,** deseeded and chopped

METHOD

1 Combine all jerk ingredients in a bowl and mix well. Add chopped vegetables and tomatoes and stir well.

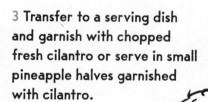

2 Place in a large pan, and cook on medium-low heat. Simmer for 10 minutes, or until all vegetables are soft, stirring occasionally to prevent sticking.

3 Transfer to a serving dish and garnish with chopped fresh cilantro or serve in small pineapple halves garnished with cilantro.

SERVES 4 | PREP TIME: 5 MINUTES | COOK TIME: 40 MINUTES
Recipe courtesy of Vegetarian Society

Fruit and Nut Salad with Chili Lime Dressing

INGREDIENTS

For the Dressing:

1 tbsp. **OLIVE OIL**

½ tsp. **SOY SAUCE**

1 tbsp. **CHILI SAUCE** (such as sriracha)

1 **LIME**, juiced

For the Salad:

3 oz. of your favorite **SALAD LEAVES** (such as baby spinach, arugula, or frisée)

½ small **ENGLISH CUCUMBER**, halved lengthwise, deseeded, and peeled into ribbons

6 oz. **FLAVORED BAKED TOFU,** cut into 1-inch cubes

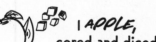

1 **APPLE,** cored and diced

¼ c. **TOASTED SEEDS** (such as pumpkin or sunflower)

1 **PEAR,** cored and diced

¼ c. mixed **ROASTED NUTS** (such as cashews or peanuts), roughly chopped

1 small **CARROT,** cut into ribbons or fine strips

¼ small **RED ONION,** sliced very thinly

To Garnish:

A few fresh **CILANTRO** leaves, roughly chopped

METHOD

1 To make the salad dressing, combine all the ingredients in a bowl and whisk together using a fork. Whisk again just before serving.

2 To serve, divide the leaves between four plates, top with the tofu, and add the rest of the salad ingredients, finishing with the seeds and nuts.

3 Just before serving, drizzle a little dressing over each salad and scatter with the cilantro.

VEGETABLES

They're not all green. Well, they are. But you know what we mean.

Vegetables are a bit heartier and typically taste more savory than fruits. Overall, they are usually what we think of when we hear the term *plant based*. Yet, like fruit, their climate-fighting power is tricky for all sorts of reasons, we learned, from the way they are grown, to where they are grown, to how they are stored and transported. There are also significant waste issues and packaging issues to consider. That said, they are low on the food chain, and that means they consume fewer natural resources than animals. As a quick choice for cool food, vegetables are an easy go-to over meat.

It takes a lot of land to raise livestock, but not so much to grow plants. Less land use is climate positive because it allows greenhouse gases to remain in the ground. Stomping on the ground kicks up CO_2 into the air. So, in a dash for cool food, hit the vegetable aisle. And if you want to up your cool food game, try expanding your culinary horizons.

> **FAST FACT:**
> Supermarkets and grocery stores typically stock fewer than fifty types of vegetables for us to choose from.

Cool Food: *VEGETABLES*

**LENTILS | PEPPERS | EGGPLANTS | SPROUTED BROCCOLI
CERTAIN PEAS* | BEANS | HEARTS OF PALM**

*such as Alaska, early snap, or southern

There are something like three hundred thousand different types of edible plant species on Earth. We eat about two hundred of them. And, as we've learned, three dominate our food supply (corn, wheat, and rice). But we're missing out on a lot of great options. Like lentils. Organic lentils are often touted as having extremely low carbon footprints because they are easy to grow and require little tending. They are technically "pulses," which are harvested for their use as dry grains.

> **FAST FACT:**
> Growing two pounds of lentils has a puny carbon footprint that amounts to driving a car about two miles.

As annual crops, they are not exactly big carbon storers because they are replanted season after season. They don't store the most carbon for years and years like giant hardwood trees do. However, for the home gardener, they're easier to grow. And they are good for the soil, and that helps sequester carbon in the ground.

Lentils are among the top climate-friendly proteins. Other pulses such as chickpeas, beans, and dry peas are also good as stand-alone cool foods or fillers, cited by numerous researchers as having the lowest carbon footprints. They are pretty easy to cook, too: you can just boil them in water.

Speaking of cooking, we had a chance to visit Sam Platt, the head of

44

the Vegetarian Society Cookery School, in the school's kitchen. The 175-year-old institution in Manchester, England, famously attended by Mahatma Gandhi, promotes vegetarianism and vegetarian cooking through chapters around the world. Platt told us that vegetarian cooking helps people make that connection between what they choose to buy, eat, and prepare and the effects that it can have on the environment.

"It's really good for people to be able to see the actual difference that one choice can make. And then if you can get them to connect, to multiply that one choice by millions of choices across the world, then there's a massive difference," Platt said. She teaches people from all walks of life how to cook with vegetarian foods. The biggest challenge isn't transitioning from meat; it's getting people to be creative and make dishes with unexpected foods.

"It's the way they're thinking about food. And in some ways, it's about being given permission to be more

FAST FACT:
One scientific team showed that replacing part of a beef burger with lentils increased its nutritional value and reduced its carbon footprint by a third.

creative with food, and particularly with vegetables and vegetarian and vegan proteins. They don't get the chance to do that generally at home 'cause they might be cooking for a family. They might be under time pressure. Also, they're often just buying whatever's in front of them at the supermarket rather than going back to mindfulness about what you buy, what you eat, and what you prepare. And that mindfulness is a remarkable change. When people find the competence of just being allowed to be creative with food, it just sparks joy. It's lovely," Platt said.

Until recently, most people came to the Vegetarian Society out of concern for animal welfare. Of course, there are religious and other health issues that drive people toward vegetarianism, but Platt has seen a shift, especially among younger members, toward adopting vegetarianism out of concern for the planet. And what makes the switch from meat to vegetable go down easier is expanding the menu of vegetarian dishes.

"If you look at the kind of recommendations for your food intake, a third of it should be vegetables. So why should we have to eat from a horrible flavor list? It's about buying better vegetables and getting people to understand that we can do exciting things with vegetables. One of the things I try—and particularly with meat reducers—to get them to understand is that there's all of these exciting things that you usually do with meat you can do with vegetables. You can marinade them. You can griddle them. You can oil brush them. You can barbecue them. You can do all these incredible things with the vegetables. And I think once people go, 'Actually,

yes, I can. They are the main part of my meal. And I, yes, I have to think about my protein and those things, but I can make the vegetables the tastiest part of my meal, as well as everything else. They're not just an extra.' That's when awakenings begin," she said.

Fruits, for example, aren't just for desserts.

"We use fruit a lot in savory dishes," she said. "You know, more often than not, they aren't the focal point of the savory dish. But they can absolutely add an element. If you look around the world, wherever fruit is grown, you'll find that it's incorporated in lots of different ways to savory dishes, as well as sweet dishes, because it's there, you

46

"Okay, I'll admit it. The rumors are true: I'm a pescatarian. That means I eat fish every now and again. I tried going all-in vegetarian—even vegan—but it just doesn't work for me. Without some animal protein, I find myself with low levels of vitamin B12, calcium, iodine, and iron. These are common deficiencies that can result from vegan diets. That's why I get (and recommend that you get) a full blood analysis to know what you might be susceptible to, and what you are lacking in terms of nutrients and the like. And, yes, in case you are wondering, I do actually need the iron that animal protein provides."

need to use it. I've seen loads of pineapple in Southeast Asian food. In the UK, we see fruit a lot in salads. We're mixing soft fruits or apples and pears with really dark peppery flavor, some leaves. They're amazing. You see it paired with traditional cheeses a lot. They are such a source of flavor and have that natural sweetness. It seems a shame to think they're just put out for a snack. Use them all the time. Don't waste them."

Adopting a cool food meal plan doesn't have to mean going completely vegetarian. Flexitarian eating is becoming popular, like veganism and vegetarianism. Flexitarian eating means being plant-centered but occasionally

ACID OR ALKALINE?

Acidity and alkaline levels are measured on a pH scale between 0 and 14. Acidic is 0.0 to 7.0, while alkaline is 7.1 to 14 on the scale. Some of the best alkaline, or basic, fruits are coconuts, grapes, apples, bananas, avocados, lemons, melons, and dates. When it comes to alkaline veggies, go for dark-green options such as spinach, kale, arugula, collard greens, mustard greens, beet greens, or watercress.

one meal. Do that frequently and the emissions saved start to add up quickly. Another benefit to cutting back on meat is health. Meats typically contain more calories than vegetables. Eating healthy, of course, can mean different things to different people. For many, healthy is opting for a more alkaline diet. Alkaline is the opposite of acidic, and some people believe a higher alkaline diet is better for our health. Whether or not there are health benefits (there are, but perhaps not as many as some alkaline advocates would have you believe), an alkaline diet is definitely good for the planet. Fruits and vegetables are considered alkaline foods along with nuts and legumes. On the other end of the spectrum are acidic foods, including meat, fish, dairy, poultry, and grains. In between are foods that contain large amounts of starch, sugar, or lots of natural fats.

We're not saying that a total alkaline diet is the way to go. But incorporating more alkaline foods into our meals or swapping out a more acidic meal for a

eating meat. (Ordering an eggplant parmesan instead of chicken parmesan, for example.) It can also mean trimming back on animal ingredients.

Take a meal like chili, and replace half the meat typically served with legumes. That 50 percent difference can cut in half the carbon emissions produced by that more alkaline meal once in a while does have huge planet potential.

Some of that information may be surprising to you. It was to us. It takes a lot of time and effort to look deeper into the health, as well as the environmental effects, of different foods. Many of the things we assume (such as dairy and grains being more alkaline) can end up being harmful to our health. When it comes to the earth's ecosystem, there are also many false assumptions. Take mushrooms. They have been hailed as food that can save the planet. But mushrooms, you also may be surprised to learn, might not necessarily be all that terrific for the environment.

Mushrooms produce (technically respire) carbon dioxide, unlike green plants that take it in and store it. We humans, of course, also exhale CO_2 when we breathe. But there are only about seven billion of us. Mushrooms are fungi, among the most abundant living organisms on Earth. According to the data, they represent 2 percent of

Better Leafy Greens than Others

- okra
- kale
- pak choi or bok choy
- red cabbage
- spinach
- watercress
- alfalfa sprouts

Earth's biomass. And while mushrooms can help forests and soils remain healthy so they can do their job of storing carbon, we learned that digging them up can further add to carbon release from the soil. When they are cultivated, the rooms in which they are grown must be kept warm, adding to their carbon footprint. Add to that the fact that mushrooms easily spoil and often end up as food waste, and their eco footprint

IT BEGAN WITH A PEA

Centuries upon centuries ago, we humans picked our vegetables in the wild. But during the Bronze Age, about five thousand years ago, we apparently decided to ditch the commute and start farming vegetables from home.

The first cultivated vegetables are thought to be peas grown in Middle Asia—India on through to Afghanistan. They were then said to be joined in other parts of the world by onions, cabbage, and lentils—among the earliest vegetables grown for us to eat. (Fruits are a different story and are dated back much farther in history.)

Likely, cultivating vegetables required a lot of trial and error. ("Try that leaf, Gilligan." Whoops. Gilligan didn't make it. Next.)

Take the classic potato, which we've talked about in this chapter. The first cultivated potato came from Peru, where the Incas domesticated the variety from a bunch of weeds. They had used the potato as a clock in order to tell time. (Surely, someone got impatient and just ate the thing.)

In the US, potatoes didn't get popular until Thomas Jefferson served them at the White House. They caught on and have become one of our most popular foods. So much so that potatoes were the first vegetable to be grown in outer space.

isn't as light as many environmentalists (like us) assumed. (The flimsy plastic packaging that many mushrooms come in is yet another waste issue.)

Another surprise comes with potatoes, sweet potatoes, and yams. They are three different things, but because they all bulk up on CO_2, the plants are expected to grow 30 percent faster in the coming years.

Potatoes, sweet potatoes, and yams are all tubers, meaning that they live belowground. They hold a lot of carbon dioxide in their organs, especially yams, which can grow as long as forty-five feet. Technically they are all perennial plants, but classic potatoes are harvested annually. Which is why sweet potatoes and yams are the cooler choices.

Sweet potatoes and yams come from different vine species but are commonly (especially in North America) bunched together as "sweet potatoes." Yet 95 percent of yams are grown in Africa, whereas sweet potatoes in the US likely come from a domestic farm. (North Carolina grows 60 percent of the crop.) Yams typically have darker and rougher skin and taste more starchy than sweet potatoes, which are more reddish and which taste, well, sweet.

Meanwhile, classic potatoes have their own identity crisis: there are more than two hundred different varieties commonly sold throughout the United States, and thousands more varieties cultivated around the world.

So what vegetables should you look for when out shopping for cool foods? To get a better idea, we turned to an organization that we admire: Plants for a Future. According to their website, it's a charity that hosts a free-of-charge online database "for those interested in edible and useful plants"—like us. PFAF has compiled a list of hundreds of

FAST FACT:
The US Department of Agriculture requires any foods with yams to also be labeled "sweet potato."

Edible Shrubs

Some of the edible shrubs that Plants for a Future lists
are part of a movement toward "carbon farming,"
which includes using more perennial plants as foods.
Here's a list of some of the perennials you can eat:

- Rose of Sharon
- Juniper
- Wolfberry boxthorn
- Wax myrtle
- Oregon grape
- Cranberry myrtle
- Bitter orange
- Golden currant
- Blackcurrant
- Gooseberry
- Ramanas rose
- Sage
- Elderberry
- American elder
- Common thyme
- Chilean guava
- High-bush blueberry

- Bilberry
- Spanish yucca
- Spoonleaf yucca
- Japanese pepper
- Trailing abutilon
- Feijoa
- Lemon verbena
- Saltbush
- Australian saltbush
- Wedgeleaf saltbush
- Indian barberry
- Pigeon pea
- Pea tree
- Tree spinach
- Yeheb
- Creeping snowberry
- Alpine wintergreen

plants that can help mitigate the problems associated with climate change. Granted, not all the plants they list are edible. However, there are a good number of vegetables that PFAF lists, along with fruits and nuts.

Unfortunately, many of the vegetables that are really good for the planet—cool foods—aren't widely available, like some of those also listed in the Future 50 Foods list at the end of this book. It's a challenge for our food system to expand the menu of environmentally friendly foods that we can easily buy. And that challenge doesn't just exist with vegetables that are grown on land. Sea vegetables, or seaweeds, are some of the best foods for capturing carbon from the atmosphere. Technically algae, seaweeds hold huge potential for mitigating climate change. In the next chapter, we'll take a look at what it might take to unlock their potential as a cool food group.

What You Can Do Today

- **Go for lentils. They are the best-in-class protein vegetable that you can eat, and they have a puny carbon footprint.**
- **Swap a high-acid meal of meats for an alkaline meal of vegetables.**
- **Going veg doesn't have to be all-in. Even splitting sandwich or taco fillings to reduce meats can make a big difference.**
- **Look for vegetables beyond the usually limited selection at supermarkets. Farmers' markets and online shopping can help expand your vegetable grocery list.**
- **Experiment with cooking different kinds of vegetables.**

Japanese Broccoli Yakisoba

INGREDIENTS
For the Sauce:

- 3 tbsp. MIRIN
- 2 tbsp. low-sodium DARK SOY SAUCE
- 2 large cloves GARLIC, crushed
- 1 small RED CHILI PEPPER (such as Fresno), finely chopped
- 1-inch by 2-inch piece fresh GINGER, grated
- 1 tbsp. CORNSTARCH, mixed with 2 tbsp. cold WATER

For the Stir-Fry:

- 2 tsp. SESAME OIL
- 4 GREEN ONIONS, sliced diagonally
- 1 CARROT, peeled and cut into matchsticks
- 1 RED BELL PEPPER, deseeded and cut into strips
- ½ lb. BROCCOLINI, trimmed and cut into three equal pieces
- 1 lb. frozen EDAMAME BEANS
- 2 packed c. shredded GREEN CABBAGE
- ¼ c. chopped vegetarian KIMCHI
- ¾ c. plus 2 tbsp. low-sodium VEGETABLE BROTH
- 10.5 oz. SOBA NOODLES, cooked as directed on the package and drained
- 1 tbsp. toasted SESAME SEEDS
- 1 RED CHILI PEPPER (such as Fresno), sliced for garnish
- freshly ground BLACK PEPPER

55

METHOD

1 Place all of the sauce ingredients into a small bowl and mix well until combined.

2 Heat the oil in a wok or large frying pan. Add the green onion, carrot, and pepper. Stir-fry for 2–3 minutes.

3 Add the Broccolini, edamame beans, cabbage, and kimchi. Stir-fry for a further 2–3 minutes.

4 Pour the sauce over the vegetables along with the broth. Gently bring to a simmer for 2–3 minutes until the sauce thickens. Add a splash of water if the sauce looks a little too thick.

5 Stir in the noodles and heat gently for 1–2 minutes until piping hot. Season with black pepper to taste.

6 Transfer the noodles to warm bowls. Sprinkle with the toasted sesame seeds and garnish with sliced red chili.

Recipe courtesy of Vegetarian Society

RECIPE

Pea, Spinach, and Goat Cheese Frittata

INGREDIENTS
For the Frittata:

3 tsp. OLIVE OIL

½ c. plus 1 tbsp. PEAS, fresh or frozen

Pinch of SALT

6 EGGS

& ground BLACK PEPPER

1 small RED ONION, sliced very thinly

1 clove GARLIC, finely chopped

⅓ c. 2% MILK

⅓ c. crumbled vegetarian GOAT CHEESE

2 packed c. BABY SPINACH

1½ tbsp. finely chopped CHIVES

For the Salad:

3 oz. SALAD LEAVES

1 tsp. OLIVE OIL

1 tbsp. LEMON JUICE

57

METHOD

1 In a nonstick, oven-safe frying pan, add 2 teaspoons of the olive oil and cook the red onion and garlic over medium heat for 5 to 10 minutes until soft.

2 Remove the pan from the heat and transfer the onion and garlic to a small bowl.

3 Add 1 teaspoon of olive oil to the frying pan, turn the heat to high, then add the spinach and peas. Cook for a few minutes until the spinach has wilted, then add the cooked onion and garlic, spreading the mixture evenly to cover the base of the pan.

4 Crack the eggs into a bowl with the milk and whisk until fully combined, then add the chives, salt, and pepper. Pour the egg mixture over the vegetables in the frying pan.

5 Heat the broiler to medium.

6 Dot the egg mixture with pieces of goat cheese and turn the heat down, leaving the frittata to cook until the egg starts to set.

7 Now place the pan under the broiler to cook the top of the frittata until it starts to brown, approximately 10 minutes.

8 Remove the frittata from the broiler and let it cool for a few minutes.

9 While the frittata is cooling, evenly divide the salad leaves between two plates and dress with olive oil and lemon juice.

10 Carefully slide the frittata onto a chopping board, slice, and serve on the plates with the salad.

SEA VEGETABLES

Seaweed is sexy. Seaweed is scum. Seaweed is something we should probably all be eating right now.

Seaweeds aren't the first food group that any of us likely think about. In fact, many of us probably don't even know that seaweeds are a food group consisting of thousands of varieties. What's so special about seaweeds? When we started working on this book, everyone we spoke with told us that seaweeds are hands down the number one cool food for the planet. And everything we've read since backs up that assertion.

Oceans absorb about a third of all the carbon pollution produced by burning fossil fuels for energy—the kind of energy the world is trying to wean itself off of for cleaner alternatives such as wind and solar power. If the world's oceans didn't trap and store carbon dioxide from the air, the average global temperature would be far hotter than it is today. And average temperatures across the world, as we know, are already smashing heat records. Which is how seaweeds come into the picture to cool things.

> **FAST FACT:**
> If just 9 percent more seaweeds were grown in the ocean, all the carbon dioxide emitted by humans could be stored underneath the sea.

HOW MANY SEAWEEDS ARE THERE?

Thousands. About 1,500 different types of brown seaweed; more than 4,000 types of red seaweed; and over 7,000 types of green seaweed. Red and brown seaweeds are the types most often used for food.

We discovered that all the different kinds of seaweed have amazing potential for storing carbon dioxide from the atmosphere, which, in turn, keeps global temperatures from rising. They're truly climate positive. They're also nutrient-rich and have lots of other health benefits. While they may not be so easy to find at your local grocery store, that's changing as more markets stock up to meet increasing demand. Ordering online (like with some of the other foods we've mentioned so far) is also an option.

Given the amazing prospects of seaweeds, we dove into the literature to learn more. Seaweeds are forms of algae, multicellular organisms that are part of the building blocks of the ocean's food chain. Like green plants on land, seaweeds use photosynthesis to capture carbon dioxide and produce oxygen. As much as 70 percent of the total oxygen on Earth, in fact, comes from the ocean.

SEAWEED'S SUPERPOWER

Photosynthesis is the process of turning sunlight, water, and carbon dioxide into oxygen. This is the superpower of most seaweeds that has been passed along through genes to most other green plants. It works like this: plants consume moisture and CO_2 from the air, and their cells convert that into glucose that it stores as energy and oxygen that is respired into the atmosphere.

Of course, the greens we grow on land are far more abundant in the vegetable section of the grocery store. In fact, they ARE the vegetable section. Yet the irony is that the lettuce, kale, cabbage, beans, sprouts, spinach, and other plants we commonly find in the produce section all started off as a form of algae, or seaweed. Like us, they began life in the ocean many millennia ago. Don't get us wrong, many land-based vegetables are great climate-positive choices, too—they're just not as powerful and effective at storing carbon as seaweeds.

Growing seaweed isn't all that difficult. Basically, sunlight and water are what's needed. In the ocean, seaweed farmers attach stalks of seaweed to ropes or nets that are left to float in the water. The seaweed grows in columns and farmers harvest it by trawling in the lines or by raking the top of the seaweed farm canopy.

Moss Landing is a little town on the seashore fifteen miles north of Monterey, California. It is about as close to the sea as you can get: it teeters on the beaches and tidal marshes that flow inland before turning into large tracts of farmland. There, Mike Graham, a phycologist (seaweed researcher and educator),

KALE VS. SEAWEED

Even when compared to the low carbon footprint of a vegetable like kale, seaweeds are still clearly a better choice. Producing a kilo of kale uses about as much energy and produces about as much CO_2 as a car driving about one-tenth of a mile. That's not a lot. But every kilogram of seaweed is the equivalent of keeping that amount stored at sea.

operates Monterey Bay Seaweeds, one of the largest seaweed farms in the United States.

"There's a lot of seaweed hype going on the planet right now," Mike told us. Out his door, just off the coast, is the patch of ocean where the world's largest kelp forest grows. Graham wants to farm that patch like crop growers do in the Salinas Valley, one of the largest agricultural centers in the country—also known as America's Salad Bowl—which is not very far down the road (the other way from the ocean) from where he lives.

Graham sells seaweeds to top chefs mostly. A small industrial building next to the large tanks where his seaweeds grow serves as his office. It's where seaweeds are tested for flavor, packed up, and shipped.

"I was not selling this as a climate-changing food alternative. I was selling this as, 'Hey, guys, I've eaten three hundred species of seaweed and it tastes really good.' Every time I go on a field trip, I eat seaweed off the rocks with my students to get them to think about different aspects of it. Plus, there's no seaweed that is toxic. I mean, some tastes bad, but none are toxic. So, I thought I had a little bit of info to give chefs that they had never had before. Kombu, wakame, and nori. Yep, that's what we eat. And here I am walking around in flip-flops and a Teenage Mutant Ninja Turtles T-shirt, going into Michelin Star restaurants with bags of seaweed going, 'Can I meet the executive chef?' And these guys come out to me and we're opening bags. And the first thing they're thinking is, 'We already have nori. We already have kombu.' I was like, 'No, no, this is different. Right?'

FAST FACT:
Because kelp—a brown seaweed—grows so big and so quickly, it captures the most CO_2 in the seas.

64

So, I've got them eating this out of the bags in the back of the restaurant."

And guess what? It does taste different. He can adjust flavors with air bubbles and temperature settings alone. It's something else: it's grown for taste.

"We have fifty of the top one hundred restaurants in the US as our clients. And they text us daily. Like today, it's going out to Eleven Madison Park," Graham said.

Different colors also mean different flavors. "There are three types of seaweeds. There are reds, there are greens, and there are browns. Greens make sucrose just like any other thing we eat. Therefore, we can eat green sea lettuce. We can just eat it. It's totally fine. Our bodies digest it. Reds and browns do not make sugars that humans can generally digest. So, it's all fiber. It's something that goes into, like, protein shakes. They literally are a filler that doesn't do much for flavor. That's what kelp is. Kelp is mostly fiber.

Grow Your Own Seaweed

You can make your own edible seaweed at home. Simply fill an aquarium with warm saltwater. Place a rock at the bottom of the tank, and attach the bottom of a seaweed strand to it. It should stick, or you can clamp it in place with another rock. Keep the water temperature at seventy-two degrees, and watch it grow! It's a fun experiment to experience its fresh taste.

The MOST Common Seaweeds

We found a dozen different types of seaweed that are among the most common to eat and that we think could easily go more mainstream. According to the Food and Agriculture Organization of the United Nations, these are the most common kinds:

Nori probably the most familiar, is purplish black and said to be among the most nutritious seaweeds. It's used to wrap around rice and made into hand or cut sushi rolls, or dried and eaten as chips.

Sea lettuce is technically a species of *Ulva* and is often mixed with two other types of seaweed to make aonori, a dry and flaky mix that is used to spread on top of miso soups and other dishes.

Kombu is dried seaweed made from long brown strands that can stretch for several feet. It's a common type to eat in Japan and is highly cultivated.

Wakame is a brown seaweed that looks like a big leaf from a tree and is mostly used in soups and noodles.

Hijiki is super dark and is cooked in stir-fries with bean curds and other vegetables.

Mozuku is a dark-brown seaweed that can be eaten as a fresh vegetable with soy sauce or used in a salad.

Sea grapes are also known as green caviar and can be pale green or yellow. They are among the more expensive seaweeds because they are handpicked from sandy sea bottoms. They are used on their own, as "caviar," or in salads.

Dulse is super popular. It's a red alga and usually comes as flakes or a powder for use as a seasoning.

Irish moss can be made into puddings or used as a garnish or a soup ingredient.

Winged kelp is said to have the best protein and is often eaten fresh.

Sea moss is sold as a "salad vegetable" in Hawaii and is sometimes served with fish.

Carola is a seaweed growing in popularity in South America. It's bright red and is eaten as a common vegetable.

Any and all of these seaweeds, or should we say, "sea vegetables," are super climate-friendly choices.

The flavor part that you're talking about is that various other seaweeds make a lot of umami. So, it's got that rich, savory flavor and a couple of other compounds that really accent food," he said.

Seaweed, he explained, can taste like chips, caviar, or something in between—nachos, even.

"We have a chip called 'Dulsitos.' Two ounces has ten grams of protein. Wow. You don't get ten grams of protein in a two-ounce bag of Fritos! Even if you did, you're going to be fighting all the guys that are doing corn and dealing with water issues and dealing with ethanol issues. So, can we sell three thousand tons of Dulsitos? I don't know, but we're making a product whose flavor is amazing. When we first started putting it out—I think it was during the Super Bowl—at a couple local bars with guys just drinking Modelos, they couldn't stop eating the chips! 'Cause the umami and the salt made them thirsty. They had no idea they're eating seaweed chips. Nowadays you go to people and say, 'Try this. It's a seaweed chip. It's good for the environment.' And they

SHADES OF GREEN

The darker a seaweed's color, the more carbon dioxide it absorbs. Green seaweeds are found closer to the surface, then brown seaweeds are lower than that, and red seaweeds are closest to the bottom of the ocean. As sunlight passes through water, different wavelengths, or what we see as color, are filtered out.

go, 'Oh.' And they taste it. They say, 'I don't know what that thing was, but it was amazing.'"

Eating more seaweed, in theory, should create more demand for it, and therefore more of it would need to be grown to feed our appetites. That growth, we figured, could help the prospects for storing more carbon dioxide in the sea, and a lot of experts say it is indeed a good bet. Of course, that would only be part of it. Consuming more seaweeds would also mean we'd be eating less of other foods that take a whole lot more energy to produce and that add to, rather than subtract from, the excess greenhouse gas problem we're experiencing with the atmosphere. So it would help cool things even more.

A telling example that we came across shows just how much greenhouse gas we could save by a simple ingredient switch: a sea lettuce salad may be as much as twenty times more effective at reducing carbon emissions than a traditional house salad made with lettuce that's been grown on land. Clearly, sea lettuce is the better choice for the earth. Yet scan the green section at the grocery store, and likely, sea lettuce is nowhere to be found. At least that was the case in the stores we visited.

If you're wondering what exactly sea lettuce is, we did the research for you. Sea lettuce is technically a kind of green algae that has ruffle-edged leaves and looks a lot like a leaf of lettuce grown in the ground. It's slightly more tart and salty tasting but similar in texture to most other leafy greens.

There's a lot to cover with seaweeds, from how they look to where they're from, how they taste, and what dishes they are used for. Seaweed farmers, chefs, and researchers gave us a boatload of information to share.

FAST FACT:
North America grows only one-thousandth of the world's supply of seaweeds.

What information stood out maybe most for us, however, was the challenge seaweeds seem to face on their name alone. "Seaweed" doesn't sound all that appetizing. Seaweed likely reminds most of us of something we've stepped on at the beach, or something icky that we have to remove from our bathing suits after a swim in the ocean. Neither one of those things really screams the word *yum*. So, to make seaweeds more appealing, there is an under-the-radar sales campaign to rename seaweeds that are grown as human food in order to foster more demand for them. "Sea vegetable" is thought to have a more palatable connotation that could help to make seaweed as a group more available at grocery stores,

restaurants, and markets. We think it's a better label, too.

As we were looking deeper into all the different types of seaweeds for this book, we learned how researchers found the oldest ancestor of all the green plants on Earth. It was discovered under a rock in northern China: a strand of seaweed. The scientists were examining ancient rocks when they found the fossilized strand. Using computer models, the researchers matched the cellular structure of algae to the modern green plants we see and eat today on land. This meant all plants could be traced back to this billion-year-old momma strand of seaweed. That made us wonder why seaweeds—which are far easier to grow than even a small cabbage patch and have obviously been around a long, long time as a food source—never really caught on in Western society, especially in America. Sure, if you're living in the Midwest, seaweeds aren't an easy grab. But on the coasts, there are lots of different seaweeds for the taking.

FAST FACT:
Seaweeds are not only more efficient at photosynthesis than land-based plants; they can grow far bigger— miles long!

70

WHEN AMERICA LOVED SEAWEED

Most of us likely only eat seaweed when dining on Asian food. Which is a shame. If more of us Americans and the rest of the world's population could eat more seaweeds and, in turn, urge more to be grown in the ocean, all the CO_2 artificially emitted in a year could be brought back to preindustrial levels, as mentioned earlier.

Seaweeds as food in the US began to rise in the last century in California and Hawaii, which claim large Asian populations. In fact, the first Japanese sushi restaurant in the United States opened in the early 1900s in Los Angeles's Little Tokyo neighborhood.

In the 1960s and '70s, when sushi gained increasingly larger popularity in the US due to pop-culture interest in Japan as a whole, with books and television miniseries like *Shōgun* forging the way, seaweed demand began to grow year after year—just not enough, apparently, to entice farmers to grow more at scale.

Then in 1977, a healthy-eating trend began to grow, prompted by the release of the McGovern Report by the US Senate (specifically a committee chaired by Senator George McGovern, hence the name). The report recommended that people consume more seasonal vegetables, seaweed, fish, and shellfish and cut back on meat, sugar, and salt. The recommendations mirrored the Japanese diet, creating a heyday for Japanese food—seaweeds included—and sushi sales soared. At the same time, Hollywood began spotlighting Japan, making sushi and even seaweeds fashionable.

Seaweeds contain several nutrients, antioxidants, and fiber without significant calories. They have probiotics that are good for gut issues and may help with digestion. They may reduce blood pressure and boost immune systems. And their antioxidants can help stabilize blood sugar, reducing the risk of developing diabetes. Of course, there are things to look out for with seaweeds, like ingesting too much iodine or heavy metals, and the possibility that its high potassium level and amount of vitamin K could interfere with the effectiveness of certain medications. Yet all in all, seaweeds have a host of health benefits.

We couldn't find a clear answer why seaweeds never became as popular as, say, spinach, even in coastal communities, beyond the fact that our cultural American diet was largely informed by the mostly land-based European diet.

Throughout Asia, seaweeds are very popular dishes or ingredients. Island nations such as Japan, with its long coastlines and access to many different types of seaweeds, made it a staple food—there, seaweeds make up more than 10 percent of what people eat.

By taste and food preference alone, seaweeds may not have the goods to rise in popularity in the West. But climate change seems to be bringing awareness of seaweed's environmental benefits and giving new rise to demand.

Whole Foods, the well-known supermarket chain, reports that shopper demand for seaweeds is a top-selling trend at its stores. And we see dried nori seaweed popping up at many places in the form of small packets as a snack. That's a good choice. But compared to the thousands of seaweed varieties, not to mention the land-based green vegetables on offer, there are slim pickings. That puts the onus on us consumers to seek out, request, and use more seaweeds in our meals. If the demand we create is heard by grocery stores, they'll stock more on their shelves. And the more that is stocked, the more that will have to be grown, capturing abundantly more carbon dioxide from the atmosphere.

Tim Flannery, one of the world's leading environmentalists, agrees that more of us should be not only familiar with seaweed's climate benefits but also using more of it in our daily lives to prop up demand. That includes eating it. He has even begun a campaign promoting seaweed farming around the globe. He believes seaweed is a key ingredient in helping to solve the climate-change crisis. We had a chance to catch up with Flannery while he was at home in Melbourne, Australia.

"Seaweed is behind a lot of things, but it's not the sort of stuff you pick up directly very much. It's going to be hidden in your toothpaste, in fillers for various foods. We're using a red seaweed as a cattle feed, and it's reducing emissions by about 98 to 99 percent. So that is a huge gain. And all you need is twenty-five grams, just a little tiny bit like that every day, and it has this massive effect," he said.

Cattle burps produce copious amounts of the harmful gas methane. There are about a billion and a half cattle on the planet. Feeding them more digestible food that quells their belches could indeed be a climate savior as the methane produced by cattle adds up to the single biggest source of greenhouse gases from agriculture.

Hence, the indirect climate potential of feeding cattle seaweed is massive, as Flannery noted. Someday, maybe, we'll even be able to purchase beef at the store that just as readily displays it as "seaweed fed" as it does "free range."

In any event, Flannery was full of

stats. For example, in his short book *Sunlight and Seaweed*, meant to complement the awareness campaign, he reported:

> Globally, around 12 million [metric] tonnes of seaweed are grown and harvested annually, about three-quarters of which comes from China. The current market value of the global crop is US$5–6 billion, of which $5 billion comes from sale for human consumption. Production, however, is expanding very rapidly. Seaweeds can grow very fast—at a rate more than 30 times that of land-based plants. Because they de-acidify seawater, making it easier for anything with a shell to grow, they are also the key to shellfish production. And by drawing CO_2 out of the ocean waters (thereby allowing the oceans to absorb more CO_2 from the atmosphere) they help fight climate change.

He went on to explain how seaweeds could also be burned and used as a natural fuel. But let's stick to talking about eating it. On that point, Flannery said that we are in the "early days" of seaweed as a trendy food like kale has become. "So, in terms of stuff that you actually pick up off the shelf, in ten years' time you'll probably have a lot more stuff on the shelf than we have now," he said. For the moment, it's on us to read our toothpaste and tablet labels more carefully to figure out which contain seaweed—and buy those to help create demand.

This all isn't to say that edible seaweed production itself isn't growing. It is. Yet these sea vegetables don't add up to much inventory and are used more as garnishes than anything mainstream. There isn't even a comparison to be made in the West between seaweeds and green vegetables in the produce section, he said; seaweeds are nonexistent. Ask a store clerk, he advised, to get more on shelves.

We in the West source most of our seaweed from Asia, where it's a staple item. The majority of the seaweeds that we eat in the US apparently come from "sea-based farms off the coasts of China, Indonesia, the Philippines, South Korea, and Japan," according to journalist Katie Fehrenbacher in *The Guardian*. Yet there is potential for other areas to step in. Flannery said, "The Bahamas and places like that, where you've got a plateau that storms can sweep seaweed into, they're all good places to grow it for sequestration purposes." Deep ocean seaweed is our best hope for plunging carbon into the depths—and keeping it there. It's where seaweed can grow the biggest and store the most CO_2 in its leafy appendages.

Interestingly, Norway is trying to muscle in on the seaweed farming business to help fight climate change and keep things cool. Alaska, which shares part of the Arctic Circle with Norway and has similar seaweed farming potential, has also begun eyeing seaweed production as a big business opportunity. We also found that Maine, Massachusetts, Florida, and parts of California are looking to get in on the entrepreneurial seaweed farming act, all in a bid to taper climate change. So in those states and regions, seaweeds may be more available at stores and restaurants. Look for them.

Kelp Forests

Kelp is a common type of seaweed with a long stalk that stretches taller than trees. The northern Pacific kelp forest makes for one of the biggest natural storage facilities for CO_2 on Earth. Maybe *the* biggest. And it produces an enormous amount of the oxygen we breathe. We have the potential to grow more forests like it—and we should.

Seaweed as a cool food is facing other challenges beyond lack of consumer demand. We can't have more seaweed if we can't keep our oceans clean. We hear a lot about plastics and other trash that end up causing massive amounts of marine pollution. Contaminants crimp the ability to grow seaweed. Fertilizer runoff and other toxic discharges also infect coastal waters and can kill marine vegetation. That's why minding our use of plastics and keeping our beaches clean is important. We can all do our part.

And climate change itself is taking a toll on seaweed health. The rise in seawater temperatures makes growing seaweeds more and more difficult. Kelp, for example, thrives in nutrient-rich, cool waters where upwelling occurs, or when

"Solutions abound. I'm no phycologist, but I wonder how surprised folks would be that seaweed alone can answer the carbon dioxide emissions dilemma. How big a task would a 9 percent increase in this ocean-grown magical material be? Part of the impetus for this project is to inspire capable individuals and the general public to take interest in the solutions.

"There was a lunch joint on West Fourth in New York City called Dojo—I remember scarfing down hijiki tofu burgers there with Matt Dillon in the '80s. So, my association with sea vegetables goes way back. I'm earmarking this challenge. Big challenge, huge upside."

colder seawater gets washed to the surface by ocean layers that overturn one another. This is prevalent in the Pacific Northwest and the reason why the area is rich in marine animals that eat or find a home in kelp forests. It's also why it apparently gets so foggy in the northern Pacific: warmer air flows over the colder surface water.

But when surface waters warm, all that goes away . . . and so does the seaweed.

Because of the challenges with farming seaweed in the wild—minding contaminants and increasingly warmer waters—some farmers have taken to growing seaweed on land in giant bins. The tanks are left open and exposed, but they can be monitored and harvested more easily. Once the chosen seaweed stalk is fetched from the ocean and placed in the tank, growth happens naturally.

To be sure, land-based seaweed farming cannot claim to store CO_2 like offshore farms, but it can help promote seaweed as a food group and help supply restaurants and specialty food stores that don't need as much product.

The good news is the more we are exposed to different seaweeds, the more we seem to like their taste and seek them out. More restaurants are putting seaweed dishes on their menus. And the more we understand the multiple uses for seaweeds— whether in our salads or for animal feed or even burning seaweed as an energy source—the more we'll have to grow and the better chance we'll have at fixing the climate.

"More seaweed please," may take a bit of getting used to saying, but the sentence could and should serve as the main course in any discussion about how to fix the climate.

While seaweeds may be a game-changing climate fixer of a food, we know they aren't for everyone. Which is why we began looking into nuts, arguably among the best cool foods birthed from soil.

What You Can Do Today

- Try different seaweeds as replacements for land-based vegetables. The most popular to eat are nori, sea lettuce, kombu, wakame, hijiki, mozuku, sea grapes, dulse, Irish moss, winged kelp, sea moss, and carola.

- Go for kelp. It grows the fastest and absorbs the most CO_2.

- Try seaweed supplements to encourage more seaweed to be farmed.

- Try growing your own seaweed to experience its fresh taste.

- Mind your litter and plastic use. Both often become ocean pollution that crimps seaweed growth.

- If you're a meat eater, look for beef that's been sourced from cows fed seaweed. These "methane-reduced" labels are likely to begin appearing in supermarkets.

Recipe courtesy of Vegetarian Society

Ocean Pie
Mushroom and Tofu Filling Flavored with Seaweed

INGREDIENTS

For the Base:

8 oz. *BAKED TOFU*

1 tbsp. *OLIVE OIL*

½ tsp. *HOT SMOKED PAPRIKA*

Splash of *SOY SAUCE*

5 *SHALLOTS*, finely sliced

2 cloves *GARLIC*, crushed

8 oz. *WHITE MUSHROOMS*, finely sliced

8 oz. *OYSTER MUSHROOMS*, finely sliced

¼ c. dried *SEAWEED* salad mix

For the Sauce:

2 tbsp. *BUTTER*

1 tsp. *FLOUR*

1½ c. *MILK*

⅓ c. plus 1 tbsp. *HEAVY CREAM*

¼ c. *PEAS*

½ c. chopped *ITALIAN PARSLEY*

1 tsp. *VEGETARIAN STOCK* concentrate

For the Topping:

1 lb. *POTATOES*, peeled and cut into chunks

3 tbsp. *MILK*

2 tbsp. *BUTTER*

A little *CHEESE*, grated

Pinch of *SALT* and *PEPPER*

79

METHOD

Preheat oven to 350°F.

For the base:

1 Slice the tofu into strips and cut diagonally along each edge. Place the tofu into a nonstick pan with a little olive oil. After 10 minutes, carefully turn over and add a dusting of paprika and a splash of soy sauce. Continue to cook for another 5 minutes. When cooked, set to one side.

2 Gently fry the shallots for 5 minutes. Once cooked, remove half and set to one side. Add the garlic, hot smoked paprika, mushrooms, and seaweed to the pan and cook on low. After 10 minutes, transfer to an ovenproof dish and add the tofu.

For the sauce:

3 In a separate pan, melt the butter, then add the flour and allow to cook for 2 minutes, stirring constantly. Add the milk, gradually stirring with a whisk. The sauce will thicken as it is brought to a boil.

4 Add the cream and parsley (reserve a little parsley for garnish), peas, reserved shallots, and 1 teaspoon stock concentrate. Adjust the seasoning to taste, then spoon the sauce over the tofu and mushroom base.

For the topping:

5 Bring a large pan of water to boil and add the potatoes. Simmer for 15 minutes until tender. Drain and mash with the milk, butter, and cheese (if using). Season with salt and pepper. The potatoes should have a light and creamy texture.

6 Spread the potatoes over the base. Bake in a preheated oven at 350°F for 20 minutes until golden and crispy. If neccessary, broil until golden on top.

7 Before serving, garnish the pie with a little chopped parsley. Serve with steamed fresh spinach.

81

Recipe courtesy of Vegetarian Society

Miso Soup with Tofu

INGREDIENTS

3 c. *WATER*

I sheet *NORI (SEAWEED)*, sliced into strips

3 tbsp. *WHITE MISO PASTE*

I large *GREEN ONION*, finely sliced

7 oz. *FIRM TOFU*, cut into small cubes

I tsp. reduced-sodium *SOY SAUCE* (optional)

METHOD

1 Boil the water in a medium-sized saucepan and add the nori. Turn the heat down and simmer for 5 minutes.

2 Place the miso paste in a small dish with a little hot water and whisk with a fork. Add the miso paste to the saucepan along with the green onion and tofu. Simmer gently for a further 5 minutes.

3 Serve in small bowls or mugs and season with a little soy sauce if you like.

NUTS

Sometimes you feel like a nut. It'd be better for the world if you felt that way more.

We're all by now used to hearing about planting trees to save the environment and offset the carbon emissions that we humans produce. The fact that trees store lots of carbon dioxide from the atmosphere is well known. But thinking about trees as a food source isn't always included in those lessons. In fact, The Nature Conservancy, an environmental organization that we called on to find out which "tree foods" we might highlight in this book, said they increasingly try to underscore the idea that preservation and food are linked and not mutually exclusive, as many people believe. Oftentimes trees are chopped down so farmers can grow crops on the cleared land. But TNC notes that forests naturally produce their fair share of food products, too—nuts being among their top stock.

There are dozens of nuts whose trees help keep vast amounts of carbon stored. Acorns are linked to the most carbon-storing power of the nut group because

FAST FACT: According to one study, certain nuts store nearly 75 percent more greenhouse gases than seasonal vegetables.

THE BIG THREE

As 60 percent of the global population's food consumption comes from three foods—rice, corn, and wheat—seems like we could afford to include more climate-positive foods like nuts.

....

they come from oak trees, which can grow to massive sizes and store tons of CO_2 in their branches, trunks, and roots. But squirrels we are not. Acorns take processing to make them digestible for people to eat, and that process adds to their carbon footprint and largely knocks them out of the box of top nut contenders as cool foods. With edible acorns in short supply, we examined lists of other contenders for top cool food nuts—nuts that we are used to seeing on the grocery store shelves and whose supply boost might

cause more planting of the trees from which they come. On that measure, the lowest carbon footprint of tree nuts is awarded to cashews, followed by pistachios and pecans. Chestnuts, walnuts, hazelnuts, macadamia nuts, and Brazil nuts were all tied in terms of their CO_2 emissions.

There are several stages to measuring a carbon footprint when it comes to trees that produce edible nuts. First, there's the tree's natural carbon sequestration—how much carbon the tree absorbs and stores. Then there are the subtractions from that—gathering, storage, processing, and transportation, which all produce carbon dioxide. These last four stages vary by the kind of nut: how the

FAST FACT:
An oak tree can store more than five tons of carbon over its lifetime, more than any other nut tree on the planet.

86

THE WORLD'S BIGGEST CASHEW TREE

More than a hundred years ago, Brazilian fisherman Luiz Inácio de Oliveira probably didn't think he'd leave such a big mark on the world. But in 1888, at a time when Jack the Ripper was roaming the streets of London, railroads were being built across the United States, China was settling from its Opium Wars, and the scramble to colonize Africa was on, Inácio de Oliveira did something relatively simple in a place far, far away from all that: he planted a cashew tree on Brazil's rugged northern coast. A few years later, at the age of ninety-three, he died while resting under the shade of its leaves. It's also where he was buried. The tree lived on, however, growing and growing and growing and growing, entering *The Guinness Book of Records* in 1994 as the world's biggest cashew tree.

Skeptics say there had been another tree on the plot—a thousand years older, at least—with which Inácio de Oliveira's tree merged. Still, the "Maior Cajueiro do Mundo" now covers more than two acres of land and produces eighty thousand nuts per year. The average cashew tree yields about two thousand nuts by comparison. It has become a major tourist attraction and food business operation. Which goes to show we don't know what impact we might have by simply planting a tree and watching it grow.

nut is gathered, whether by hand or machine; whether it needs to be stored in a refrigerated or heated container; whether said nut needs to be treated or processed before it's consumed; and how far it has to travel before it lands on a store shelf. The more energy used in any of these stages, the more emissions created that add to the climate-change problem. Researchers, scientists, and analysts painted different pictures for us of how carbon footprints can vary based on the emissions produced in all of these steps. This is why the climate friendliness of supply chains needs to be examined so closely.

The biggest carbon footprint of commonly eaten nuts goes to almonds. (Even though they are cool, they are not as cool as other tree nuts.) The raw material extraction, processing, and manufacturing phase of almond production apparently creates a lot of CO_2 emissions relative to how much carbon the nuts sequester.

Separate consideration also needs

Cool Food: NUTS

CASHEWS | BRAZIL NUTS | ALMONDS | HAZELNUTS
MACADAMIA NUTS | PECANS | PISTACHIOS | WALNUTS
ACORNS | CHESTNUTS | BEECHNUTS

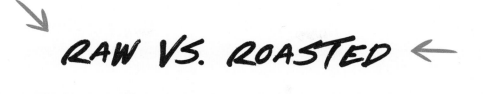

RAW VS. ROASTED

Medical experts praise the nutritional benefits of both raw and roasted nuts, and both have their pros and cons. Let's see how they compare:

RAW NUTS	**ROASTED NUTS**
PROS	**PROS**
• Fewer calories • Less sodium	• More flavorful • Easier to digest
CONS	**CONS**
• Less flavorful/tasty • Harder to digest	• Higher in sodium • Require more energy to produce

Because roasting involves producing more energy—and that dings the climate—raw nuts, on the cool food scale, are the better choice.

to be given to the water footprints of nuts, as well as other environmental and social issues, such as the kind of labor used in farming and collecting them. Many nuts come from developing countries where poor labor conditions exist. (This, we're told, is often the case with cashews.)

Another consideration when it comes to nuts is allergies as tree nut allergies are among the most common food allergies. Walnuts, almonds, hazelnuts, pecans, cashews, and pistachios are the source of the most common allergic reactions. And we learned why being allergic to one kind of nut often means being allergic to others: nut proteins can bind to specific antibodies in a person's immune system and trigger immune defenses. These reactions can be mild or deadly!

Interestingly, one of the most popular "nuts," and the source of many allergies, isn't even a nut. Peanuts, despite their name, are actually legumes. They grow underground, and when they are harvested, all that soil disturbance adds

Edible Seeds

Seeds have an extremely low carbon footprint, even lower than many nuts. But while many of us munch on sunflower or pumpkin seeds and use flaxseeds, chia seeds, hemp seeds, and sesame seeds in our shakes as well as food toppings, they are better thought of for our personal health than the health of the planet. Here's why: most edible seeds come from small plants, which don't pack the carbon-storing punch of large trees. An oak tree, for example, captures and stores ten times more carbon dioxide than a flax plant.

to their carbon emissions, releasing the carbon that has been stored in the soil.

So, an easy and quick choice for a better climate is to go for tree nuts, such as the ones we have been covering in this chapter, instead of legumes like peanuts. Tree nuts produce less greenhouse gas per gram of protein than groundnuts because of all the carbon that is kept stored in them versus the carbon that is released from the ground when legumes are dug up.

More varieties of nuts can and should enter the food system. The cool news for us is the finding that most shoppers (some 60 percent) have sustainability in mind when they make their purchases.

We're focusing mostly on what we commonly brand nuts, or "culinary nuts," born from trees that store more carbon than their shrub cousins. But there are other perennial nutlike foods, such as mesquite pods, that are less well known yet good at carbon storing.

The awareness of all the benefits nuts hold has been growing in the US population for a while as well, it seems. Over the past fifty years, nut consumption has tripled. Nuts and seeds are especially good sources of protein, fiber, and heathy fats. They are low in carbohydrates, too, which makes them a great food source.

Nuts are being used as plant-based food ingredients for burgers, meats, butters, protein bars, and milk replacements. The market is soaring, and we can do even more to encourage it. Take milk made from nuts: it produces about 75 percent less carbon pollution than milk made from a cow even if that cow lives nearby and the route from its udder to our mouths is shorter than a nut gathered from a tree planted on a different continent. Cows don't, of course, store carbon dioxide

FAST FACT:
Globally, 90 percent of the people on the planet still aren't eating enough nuts.

like plants do. Rather, they consume tons of resources, such as plants, for food that would otherwise act as carbon sinks. Moreover, as mentioned in the last chapter, they are gassy, and the methane they produce significantly adds to the greenhouse gases in the atmosphere, warming the planet.

We found people are coming up with some other pretty innovative ways to eat more nuts, including Linda and Scott Neuman, who run Neu Mana Hui Farm in Kauai, Hawaii.

"We're the only commercial cashew farm of any scale in the United States," they told us.

"Everyone knows what a cashew nut tastes like, but few people know what cashew apples look like, never mind taste like. We were on a trip to Costa Rica when we first saw one. It was in an orchard, and we had the land in Hawaii, and we said, 'We could grow that. It's a similar climate,'" Linda recalled. That was twenty years ago.

On ten acres in an agronomic slice of paradise, they now have a large orchard of cashew apple trees and have developed a holistic approach to growing and processing cashews. It's a beautiful spot on the windward side of the island, which goes by the nickname "the Garden Island" because it's so lush. Neu Mana Hui Farm is set among other farms in the area that grow fruits and vegetables. With cliffs that drop steeply down to the ocean and a scenic mountainous inland, it seems like a place you could get used to living in real quick.

"What we do is we harvest, we dry. We steam under pressure, which eliminates that oil. [Cashew shells famously contain a toxic oil.] Then we let them dry some more for a couple of days, and I run them through a cutter. And that's how you open them," explained Scott.

How Many Nuts Should You Eat a Day?

The recommended daily portion of nuts is thirty grams. What does that look like for most of us who don't weigh our food before we munch? Here's the equivalent to thirty grams for each kind of nut, according to *Taste* magazine:

- 20 to 30 almonds

- 10 Brazil nuts

- 15 cashews

- 20 hazelnuts

- 15 macadamia nuts

- 40 peanuts

- 15 pecans

- 30 pistachios

- 10 walnuts

- 2 tablespoons of pine nuts

TOXIC SHELLS

It's illegal to sell cashews in their shells. The shells contain a toxic oil called urushiol, which is also used to produce military weapons. Cashews are roasted to remove the chemical and make cashews edible. Despite that processing, cashew trees store a lot of carbon naturally, which maintains their cool food factor.

The nuts are housed inside a shell—which they call a testis—that in turn is housed inside an apple.

"Removing the nut from the shell is where the hard work comes in," Linda said. "I do them by hand. The seed is removed. And then that testis is like a peanut, you know, the peanut shell, that's the testis. So that is removed and then that's your raw nut. I see people mistakenly go and buy what they think is raw. Right, well, they're always cooked once, right? Most of the big producers dip them in a hot oil. That's what makes them crunchy brown. We don't. We use a hydrated roast, and it gives a lot better outcome. It's also how you don't get a polluting problem." Burning oil causes noxious air pollution.

The nuts themselves are just one product the Neumans sell. Affecting a voice to sound like Forrest Gump, Scott said, "We have cashews, cashew butter, cashew gum, cashew candy, cashew rollups . . ."

The interest in cashew nuts as milks, butters, and alternative products has made demand soar.

The fruit is something else. "As Westerners, we really can't place the taste. It's not part of our palate. People can't even describe it, but they love it," Scott said.

The problem with cashew fruit is that it spoils quickly—after just a few days. "So there is a shelf life problem. That's why you don't see cashew fruit at the market," Linda said.

They're speaking with the state of Hawaii about possibly increasing cashew production there. (The only other US state with the right climate for cashew growing is Florida.)

"Even if it's just a tree or two, people can grow cashews themselves in the right conditions," Scott said. He's passionate about cashews' benefits: "They stabilize soil. Once you get them to maturity, they're drought tolerant. They also are a habitat for animals. Beyond even the nut, the trees are beautiful, and they offer these other things." Which is why he recommends organic cashews grown on small farms like theirs or from a botanical collection.

Linda added that cashew tree flowers attract bees and that they also produce honey from that. "A lot of people don't realize the interaction between bees and plants," she said. Cashew flowers need bees to help them pollinate and grow.

The Neumans use the apple. They use the nuts. They plant complementary crops like vanilla. They care for the soil. It, too, makes the trees grow better and faster. "It's about caring for the environment so you can appreciate it," Linda said. To that end, they want to raise awareness and get more people to understand the benefits of cashews that are grown sustainably.

"Compared to that of an orange, a cashew apple has really, really high nutritional value and all these other things that we don't necessarily promote because you get a little bit of a disconnect between the nut and the apple," Scott said. They're hoping they can change that with cashew candy like gummies and jellies.

Sweet.

The more we dug around in the nut scene—oh, yes, there is a nut scene!—the more we found that the nuts we find at the store come from some very unexpected places. We get most of our mixed nuts from Mexico. Almonds are mostly from California; hazelnuts, Turkey and Oregon; macadamias, Hawaii; pecans, Georgia; pine nuts, Russia; pistachios, California, Arizona, and New Mexico; walnuts, California; and chestnuts, China, Bolivia, Turkey, and South Korea.

Another way to keep nuts cooling the planet is to buy them and leave them where they grow. You may be wondering how that works. Let's take the macadamia nut as an example. The vast majority of macadamias can be traced to a single tree in Queensland, Australia. But as we've noted already, the commercial production of macadamias mostly exists in Hawaii. That said, we found out that the small country of Malawi in Africa is making a play to get in on the export market by promoting the carbon-capturing benefits that macadamias have.

The Neno Macadamia Trust encourages the planting of macadamia nut trees to offset the carbon produced elsewhere. It offers a program where people can purchase certificates that help small farmers plant trees, and the nuts become a sustainable food source for the local community in Malawi. The certificate holder can offset his or her own carbon emissions this way. The trust has a calculator to help figure things like how much carbon a person emits a year through flights or by driving. Matching these totals to how many trees need to be planted to offset those carbon amounts turns into some planet-friendly math. In a poor country like Malawi, these trees also provide a source of nutrition—macadamia nuts are very high in oil and high in fiber, minerals, nutrients, and vitamins—when food supplies run low, as they often do. That program certainly seems climate smart to us.

96

Given all the different places around the world where nuts are grown and harvested, transportation issues become significant. Keeping nuts local when possible is a good goal.

To that end, we were introduced to the Slow Food Foundation, which encourages growing and buying healthy food like nuts closer to home. It raises awareness of foods that may be overlooked, misunderstood, or disappearing through its Ark of Taste program, which catalogs indigenous foods, as well as via Earth Markets, which help expand the audience for local products offered for sale. The organization underwrites an array of educational resources that can go a long way toward fostering demand. It thinks of itself as more of a movement than an organization and states its mission is to "prevent the disappearance of local food cultures and traditions, counteract the rise of fast life and combat people's dwindling interest in the food they eat, where

WHAT ARE THE MOST POPULAR NUTS?

Almonds and walnuts. They make up half of all nut production. Yet pistachios are the fastest-growing nut in terms of popularity. People are eating three times as many pistachios as they did a decade ago.

it comes from and how food choices affect the world around us." If you want to learn more about slow food (versus the fast food we're used to), SlowFood.com is a good place to start.

Beyond the buy-local effort is the need to plant local. Sometimes this gets lost in the discussion, but it's super critical in the fight against climate change. This means planting trees where they belong and not, say, a palm tree in Brooklyn.

Planting nonindigenous tree species can even have a negative consequence on the climate because these trees can destroy the soil, hampering its ability to soak up copious amounts of carbon. Healthy soil stores more carbon because it contains lots of organic matter (technically soil organic matter, or SOM). This laps up carbon dioxide from the atmosphere, whereas degraded soil crimps the amount of SOM available to keep carbon in the ground. Non-native species also can die more easily, deleting the purpose of planting trees, to begin with. Which is why we should all be buying local and ensuring that the food source is a local native, too.

Take cashew nuts. We import most of them from Vietnam, Thailand, and India even though we can grow cashew trees in Florida or Hawaii. Check the packaging for where your nuts come from. The bigger the tree and the closer to home the better. For example, if you're buying cashews, and there are different brands available, choose the one that says, "grown in California," over the one "grown in Thailand."

To learn more about eating food from trees and plants that thrive close to home, we spoke with Dr. Alex McAlvay, one of America's leading botanists. His research focuses on food through time—how cultures around the world, for much of history, have figured out how to eat and not tank the planet. He told us, "I think it will have to be a combination of looking back to how our ancestors grew food, looking laterally, looking horizontally to how other cultures grow food, and then looking forward and not being too caught up or dogmatic about any of them."

Dr. McAlvay curated the science exhibit *Sowing Resilience: Origins and Change in Agriculture*, a component of New York Botanical Garden's exhibition *Around the Table: Stories of the Foods We Love*. The botanical garden is a New York City gem. It's a 250-acre site where you'd be hard-pressed to believe that you're in the

"I am somehow just now realizing how integral to my diet nuts are. When I am working on set, I'm a fiend for spicy nut mixes. When I make my breakfast shake, I grab the almond milk. My cheeky midnight snack? A couple of scoops of almond butter. Turns out I owe them a lot. While I'm happy about making my daily thirty grams of nuts, what's even more exciting is how these plants could influence the future of farming with the indigenous practices of the past. Food production, soil rejuvenation, and carbon sequestering can all happen with proper native plant choices and organic farming practices. Even with all-out technological advancement, sometimes you just need to look at the practices that have worked for centuries. Now pass me the cashew candy—hold the shell."

Bronx. There are running streams and ponds and gardens galore. Every color imaginable seems to be growing, whether on shrubs, plants, trees, or flower beds. In the education center here, McAlvay conducts much of his research.

"My work as an ethnobotanist is looking and seeing what we can learn from cultures that got it right, realizing that we don't necessarily need to leap towards the techno fix. We don't need to reinvent container gardening because we have no other alternatives. All of these things can help. But the idea is that people have developed locally adapted food systems over thousands and thousands of years, and they've undergone climatic change, they've undergone extreme weather events, and they've persisted, or we wouldn't be here today," McAlvay said.

He had sound advice for what we can do to eat well while being mindful of the planet and our increasingly dwindling food supply.

"In the US, people are struggling with drought and trying to grow their broccoli, but miles away you can find feral brassica, which is also called wild kale. It's the same species, it's wild broccoli growing on its own, but people don't harvest it because it's not grown by farmers. It's nutritious and it's delicious. Another example is out here in the tristate area: people grow spinach, but spinach has a lot of challenges right now. You go and see farmers ripping out lamb's-quarter, ripping out amaranth, ripping out field mustard—all things that are equally good or better than spinach and as nutritious or more nutritious to try and grow rather than this thing that doesn't want to grow there," he said.

He suggested wild foraging or perusing websites that feature foods that have been foraged in the wild. There are loads of options, including classes and online marketplaces.

Another suggestion is for urban planners: "Edible ornamentals that are

100

already our street trees or are in our gardens that people don't eat. These are perennial edible plants like serviceberry or dogwood, or strawberry trees, or any number of nuts. It would be, it seems, an easy choice for urban planners to just switch what plants they landscape with for these. There are plenty of native and naturalized perennials that do really well, are pretty, and would just provide a huge amount of food for cities," McAlvay said.

That's smart. Walk down the street, pick some nuts off a tree, and be on your way? In urban landscapes where there are food deserts, this seems like a simple way for cities to do more than symbolically plant trees to help the environment; it's a way to feed their populations.

Of course, growing your own garden is huge, he said. "Becoming a member of Seed Savers Exchange or one of these other networks is really enlightening and can get you involved," he said. "You sign up and you get a list of people all around the world who have different crops,

FAST FACT:
A single mature strawberry tree can offset the carbon dioxide produced by the energy the typical American household uses over the course of a week.

different varieties, and you can, just for the price of postage, request for them to send seeds to you."

The thing McAlvay encourages most is to look at food as a connection to other people, places, and things all around the world. "In terms of carbon—because it's not an individual plant, it's the whole ecosystem—you can put your money towards those things that help the continuation of people. You know, for example, a lot of tribes in the US have projects where you can buy food they produce—wild rice harvested by Anishinabek people in the Great Lakes, or hickory nuts from the Tuscarora, Indigenous people in Upstate New York. Or in

Arizona, you can buy chili peppers, pin peppers, and acorns, edible acorns. So, supporting those indigenous kind of entrepreneurial endeavors that really encourage regenerative and low carbon ecosystems can be one big way to help the planet," he said.

This is all not to ignore innovation. "We're at a point technologically where we could do some really innovative mash-ups of traditional systems. Using robots, for example. The corn, beans, and squash—Three Sisters system—has clear agronomic benefits, right?" he asked rhetorically.

Native Americans use a growing system called Three Sisters to produce healthier soils, which store more carbon. Three Sisters growing is a stacked way to plant and harvest: corn stalks provide support for beans to grow, which draw nitrogen into the ground. Squash, with its prickly leaves, provides shade and mulch and helps to ward off pests.

He said, "For farmers the beans provide nitrogen, the corn provides a stalk, et cetera, et cetera. The challenge of scaling that up has always been mechanization. You can't drive a tractor through a corn, bean, and squash field and get everything right. But are we not there with robots? We can get robots that can do a lot of different things, and they can't tell a corn from a squash and pick it? I'm not suggesting that someone make a trillion dollars on that idea. But I don't think that we have the same excuses we did fifty years ago for not reembracing these traditional methods."

In other words, ancient methods grown anew will no doubt be coming to a store near you. Someone will want to make a trillion dollars.

Eating more nuts is an excellent way to encourage more trees to be planted. But it's not the only way, as we'll see in our next chapter.

What You Can Do Today

- Incorporate more nuts into your diet. The recommended daily amount of nuts you should eat is thirty grams.

- Focus on cashews, pistachios, pecans, chestnuts, walnuts, hazelnuts, macadamia nuts, and Brazil nuts.

- Choose raw nuts over their roasted option.

- Use nuts as a good source of fiber and healthy fats.

- Consider purchasing carbon offsets in tree nut farms to balance your personal carbon emissions and help feed a local community.

- If you can buy nuts from local growers, then do that.

Cashew Butter Cookies

INGREDIENTS

½ c. UNSALTED CASHEW BUTTER

⅓ c. MAPLE SUGAR

1 tsp. VANILLA EXTRACT

⅛ tbsp. fine SEA SALT

¼ c. chopped RAW CASHEWS (optional)

⅓ c. 1-to-1 GLUTEN-FREE FLOUR blend
(e.g. Bob's Red Mill), or substitute oat or wheat flour, if desired

½ tsp. BAKING POWDER

1 tbsp. NONDAIRY MILK

METHOD

1 Preheat oven to 325°F, and line a cookie sheet with parchment paper or a silicone mat.

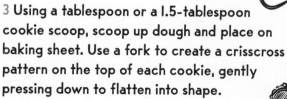

2 In a mixing bowl, stir together the cashew butter, sugar, vanilla, salt, and cashews until thoroughly combined. Add the flour and baking powder and mix well until no visible flour remains. The dough will be very dry and thick. Add the milk and mix again until it has been fully absorbed.

3 Using a tablespoon or a 1.5-tablespoon cookie scoop, scoop up dough and place on baking sheet. Use a fork to create a crisscross pattern on the top of each cookie, gently pressing down to flatten into shape.

4 Bake 10 to 12 minutes, keeping a close eye on the cookies near the end. Cashew butter tends to burn quickly and easily, so a bit less done is better than overdone in this case. The cookies will be soft straight out of the oven. Immediately sprinkle with flaked sea salt, if using. Allow cookies to cool on the baking sheet for about 5 minutes, then slide the entire sheet onto a cooling rack.

5 Allow to cool completely before storing in an airtight container.

*Pinch of flaked sea salt (optional)

105

Cashew Stir-Fry with Puffed Amaranth

INGREDIENTS

2 **LIMES**, juiced

¼ c. **VEGAN FISH SAUCE** (check your local Asian supermarket)

¼ c. gluten-free **SOY SAUCE**

2 tbsp. **COCONUT SUGAR**

½ c. **CASHEWS**

8 oz. organic, non-GMO **TOFU**, cut into 1-inch-by-1-inch pieces

1 small **RED ONION**, sliced

1 **LEMONGRASS** stalk, trimmed and bruised

½ **RED BELL PEPPER**, finely sliced

1 **CARROT**, thinly sliced

1 bunch **BROCCOLINI**

PEPPER, to taste

1 tbsp. **OIL OF CHOICE**

AMARANTH, to taste

METHOD

1 Preheat oven to 350°F.

2 Whisk lime juice, vegan fish sauce, soy sauce, and coconut sugar in a small bowl and set aside.

3 Bake tofu for 15 minutes.

4 Add red onion and lemongrass to a wok over high heat and stir-fry with oil until onion softens. Add bell pepper, carrot, and Broccolini, and cook until tender. Then add the sauce, cashews, and baked tofu pieces.

5 Sprinkle with pepper and adjust sauce to taste.

6 To "pop" the amaranth, preheat a pot over medium-high heat for 5–7 minutes. Then add the amaranth one tablespoon at a time. The seeds should begin popping imminently. Shake the pot around to avoid burning while the grains pop.

7 Serve stir-fry in bowls with prepared amaranth.

107

SYRUP

It's what's inside that counts. Syrup, we mean. Pour it on.

Without having to be felled, dug up, or otherwise killed off, big trees can be good food providers beyond fruit and nuts, we learned. We just have to know what to look for and how to get the most out of them.

Maple trees are one of the best options, being giant hardwood trees that can reach 150 feet or more in height. They grow fast, too. Red maples can stretch two feet in a year. And all that growing captures carbon pollution and keeps it stored in those tall trunks, not to mention the long and thick roots that keep them standing. Maples and other hardwoods keep it there for a long time—hundreds of years in many cases. Science tells us that carbon stays locked up inside trees until they die and decompose. Then that carbon is released back into the atmosphere and the carbon cycle begins again. CO_2 stays in the air for between 300 and 1,000 years until it can be drawn back down into trees, the ocean, or other carbon eaters.

FAST FACT: A single maple can sequester twenty-five thousand pounds of CO_2 in its lifetime, or about 50 percent more than the average US home emits in a year.

So how do we encourage more of these trees to be planted? That starts with sourcing things like food products that will appeal to the masses and boosting demand for more tree foods while at the same time conserving and growing more forests.

The most popular hardwood tree food is syrup, especially maple syrup—the most popular kind in the world. Syrup is a solution made of sugar and water. That much we knew. Of course, it's also naturally sustainable: trees only need to be tapped, not felled, for sugar to ooze. It should be pure, and it should be organic.

So, on the surface, syrups from these large hardwood trees seemed like the perfect cool food. And they do have a lot of cool food benefits—keeping forests intact and not needing much care beyond what nature serves. But to make syrup that we can all consume at scale—not just drips and drabs for a sweet taste—lots of heat (and that means energy) is needed. We found that this spikes syrup's carbon footprint and amounts to burning about three gallons of oil for every gallon of syrup produced. Still, the natural storage power of a maple tree keeps thousands of pounds of greenhouse gases from floating in the air. And that rolls back all the energy and pollution created during the syrup process and makes maple syrup (and other syrups that come from big trees) cool food.

We learned that trees start producing sap in the summer when they begin producing starch. The starch gets stored in the tree for winter and gradually converts into sugar (sucrose). When springtime rolls around, the sap begins to thaw and drip out of the tree. That's also when trees can be tapped.

Maple Syrup Grades

Maple syrup is largely divided into four color and flavor classes. All of these are classified as "Grade A."

Golden	**tastes delicate.**
Amber	**tastes rich.**
Dark	**tastes robust.**
Very Dark	**tastes strong.**

The first syrups of the season are generally lighter in color. Syrups get darker as the season progresses when more and more bacteria compound with tree sap.

The International Maple Syrup Institute told us there are four criteria for judging maple syrup: density, color, clarity, and flavor. And there is a grading system for pure maple syrup (note the word *pure*; that's important). Generally, maple syrup is graded by color alone because color tells pretty much everything there is to know about

FAST FACT:
Syrup is made from boiling sap. The heat evaporates the water that is naturally embedded in sap and leaves a concentrate—syrup!

the kind of maple syrup you're looking at. The darker the syrup, the stronger the flavor. It also tells you when the maple trees were tapped.

"We need to do a better job talking about the climate benefits of maple," Allison Hope, the executive director of the Vermont Maple Sugar Makers' Association, told us.

"Everybody else is trying to buy carbon credits, and here we are in the woods of Vermont taking care of things, and it already is happening naturally. We're not an airline out there trying to buy carbon credits to offset our footprint. We're helping offset other people's footprints," she said.

FAST FACT:

A typical chocolate candy bar has a carbon footprint of nearly ten times that of the equivalent amount of maple syrup, according to the MyEmissions.green "foodprint" calculator.

It was June, and she was in her kitchen—a couple of jars of syrup samples in front of her. It turned out to be a good time to speak with any maple grower because it's the offseason. June is also a month when Vermont comes alive with vegetation that sweeps the state until fall, when its famous foliage begins, along with the hidden makings of maple sugar inside the trunks of trees.

Hope said that maple growers such as herself know that they do the forest a world of good and that helps reduce the effects of climate change. Yet they don't market themselves that way. They've traditionally just marketed themselves on the merits of their products.

"The conversation we need to have is talking about the climate benefits of maple as a natural sweetener and the benefits of a product that requires us to take care of the earth," Hope said.

There's a symbiotic relationship between forest management and maple production. "You get out of it what you put into it. And so, really taking care of your forest, really making sure that it's a diverse landscape for other species, really paying attention to your forest management plan and taking care of those best practices, means that you're going to get better yield," she said. And better maple.

The sugar from the maple tree goes beyond syrups. Other pure products are candy, which often people will put into molds; raw maple sugar, which is like a granulated version of what we traditionally consider sugar (from sugarcane); and maple cream (which you should store in the fridge so it doesn't separate). These are all made from the same sap. It's the boiling temperature of the water that turns the sap into different products, whether syrup, granulated sugar, or candy.

Hope said, "There are so many ways to use all of those products, and those are just the pure ones. Folks have value-added products all over the place. There are maple ketchups and barbecue sauces—you name it. Folks have come up with recipes for and are selling all sorts of things." That includes athletic drinks and coffees and kombucha-like tonics.

Maple and other hardwood tree sap can also be made into sugar crystals and other forms that are far, far better choices for personal health and the planet than high-fructose corn syrup (HFCS), which is prevalent as a sweetener in many sodas and many processed foods because it's inexpensive and easy to produce. We were surprised to learn that the average American, whether they know it or not, consumes nearly forty pounds of HFCS a year. Maple syrup? Less than a pound.

No matter the product itself, Vermont maple tastes different. "Vermont specs for syrup require that it's boiled to a higher density than other states. And so, for some people that makes a difference in terms of mouthfeel. The viscosity of it, the way it feels in your mouth, is different based on

A HEALTHY ALTERNATIVE

Maple's health benefits are also plentiful. It has fewer calories than honey and is high in nutrients like riboflavin, zinc, magnesium, calcium, and potassium, according to nutritionists.

that density. I happen to think we make the best syrup in the world," she said.

Maine, New York, and other states in the Pacific Northwest are also getting into the maple syrup business. Canada, of course, is the biggest producer. The soil here or there may make the maple sap and sugar taste different. So too might the process of turning that into syrup or another product. And they all provide a valuable benefit for the climate.

Increased consumption may be one of the biggest supporters of afforestation, or new tree planting, in addition to spotlighting the dual purpose that trees can play in feeding us and converting our pollution into oxygen. And that support even comes in a bottle.

On the practical side of things, Hope said don't be quick to throw that bottle away: "The one thing that science shows us is that the color of maple darkens over time. So, if you started with what used to be the grade A fancy syrup, which is just now the light golden syrup, if it's in a plastic container, oxygen can get into that. And so, oxygenation will not harm the syrup. It will just darken the color. Beyond that, if you have an unopened container of maple, you can just leave it in your cupboard and it's fine. And once you open it, just throw it in the fridge."

Maple keeps.

▲ ▲ ▲ ▲ ▲ ▲ ▲ ▲ ▲

114

THE LEGEND OF MAPLE WATER

"Many centuries ago, during a period of food scarcity, a Native American noticed a squirrel full of energy. He watched the animal drink 'water' from a maple tree and realized it was the source of the critter's vitality. From then on, maple water, or sap, started to be consumed as a fortifying drink," or so says the website for the Quebec Maple Syrup Producers.

We're raising an eyebrow, too. But it's a good story, so why don't we stick with it. The Producers say maple's association with Canada's national pride comes from Jacques Cartier, the Frenchman who is credited with "discovering" and naming Canada in the mid-1500s when he mapped the Saint Lawrence River Basin. Cartier learned of maple water from the Native Americans and introduced the sweet taste of maple to Europe, where it became a super popular drink.

115

Maple syrup is historically a North American thing. We in the States likely associate maple trees with Vermont, but maple syrup is more Canada's child. Quebec produces the majority of the world's maple syrup, according to the data. And Canada has rather fanatically embraced its love of maple. So much so that the country uses an image of a maple leaf on its national flag.

The US Forest Service lists the silver maple as the best tree for carbon capturing. Researchers calculate the silver maple traps twenty-five times more carbon than cherry and plum trees. That's a single tree. Imagine what a forest of them could do. Which is why maple syrup could be a climate-change solution. Vermont's trees alone absorb 50 percent of the entire state's carbon emissions each year. More trees equal more emissions grabbing. And that likely equates to more maple syrup, too.

But we're losing, not gaining, maple and other mature trees every year. For instance, Vermont alone averages about 1,500 acres of forest lost yearly. And the research shows that over the past two decades, the United States has lost about 15 percent of its tree cover. That equates to some 17.4 billion tons of carbon dioxide emissions, which is nearly half of the entire world's annual total.

Despite the widespread acknowledgment that deforestation is bad for the planet, it still happens. In fact, the millions of acres of forest that are lost every year around the world—about thirty soccer fields per minute—are removed due to commercial chopping. Wood is used to build our homes and furniture, manufacture paper,

FAST FACT:
Medical experts say high-fructose corn syrup can cause health issues if eaten in large amounts. Try maple as a replacement.

116

The *MOST* Popular Syrups around the World

According to the TasteAtlas, here are the most popular syrups in the world:

Maple, as we've said, is from maple tree sap and is popular in North America.

Rheinisches Zuckerrübenkraut is made from sugar beets and is popular in Germany.

Suikerstroop is also made from sugar beets and is popular in the Netherlands.

Maltose is made from rice, wheat, corn, and barley and is popular in China.

Falernum is made from different spices and sugars and is popular in the Caribbean.

Soumada is made from almonds and is popular in Greece.

Orgeat is also made from almonds and is a popular syrup in France.

Mizuame is made from rice and is popular in Japan.

Algarrobina is made from the sap of the carob tree and is a popular syrup in Peru.

and more. If trees aren't chopped responsibly, forests disappear. Maples, along with many other tree species, suffer from our timber, pulp, and paper appetites.

Climate change is making maple trees grow slower, too. If you thought that last drizzle of maple syrup took forever to get from the bottom of the bottle to the spout, wait until you get a load of this: maple trees are projected to grow 40 percent slower because of warmer temperatures and the resulting loss of snow on the ground in New England. Ground snow insulates maple trees and helps them grow.

Extreme climate change, in other words, is killing off one of nature's biggest defenders of a temperate world. Can we eat to make the destruction stop? The simple answer is yes. If tree farmers see better prospects in tapping instead of tearing down forests, more trees can be saved and more trees planted. That helps to mitigate climate change and rising temperatures.

With maple trees in the cross hairs, we talked to Andy Finton, the landscape conservation director at The Nature Conservancy, a global environmental organization that works "to tackle the dual threats of accelerated climate change and unprecedented biodiversity loss."

"Sugar maples are my favorite tree," he said. "I'm a tree guy, but I pick sugar maple as my favorite if I had to pick one. I love chatting about maples. They're an iconic New England tree."

Finton lives just outside Boston, and his enthusiasm for sugar maples stems from the fact that they serve a dual purpose—feeding the planet with water, soil, and oxygen while at the same time providing a food source for people to consume. And as the existence of maples is threatened, so in turn are we and the planet.

His office is filled with books. And while he's clearly an intellectual, he doesn't speak flat or droll on with facts and figures. He's alive with passion and

"The end of maple syrup? In researching this chapter, I ran across an article from the Vermont Audubon Society that warns just such a thing could happen if climate change continues to push temperatures higher, forcing maple production farther north and into tighter windows. Vermont, Maine, and New Hampshire could see maple production rates dwindle. How sad. A stack of pancakes covered in maple syrup before hitting the ski slopes in Vermont was and hopefully will continue to be a part of my life.

"Maple sugar makers have apparently been adapting to a shifting climate for some time, dealing with a quicker spring arrival and testing their sapping skills. But there is only so much time that can be tightened before production suffers too much.

"Syrup makers are clearly doing what they can to keep our syrup tastes alive. What can we do? According to the Audubon Society: 'Find another reason to love maple syrup!'"

119

The Tree Lover's Stamp of Approval

The Forest Stewardship Council (FSC) label on tree products means that the forests from which the product was produced are managed responsibly. The certification comes with standards that mean trees are maintained as a sustainable resource. In short, as the FSC itself says, by choosing products with the FSC label, you are helping to take care of the world's forests.

purpose because he sees how a different future can be brought about if we simply make the forests our partners in the fight against climate change—our food partners.

Finton said, "Maple is a bit of a finicky species. It really has very specific climate requirements. It needs cool, moist forests, deep soils. And so, it's more vulnerable to climate change than some other species. For instance, some oaks are heartier, even red maple—sugar maple's close relative—is more adaptable and lives in more diverse environments. Every red maple is a generalist. It can live in wetlands. It can live on the top of a dry mountaintop, but sugar maple needs those cool, moist conditions to persist. From a vulnerability standpoint, it's really predicted that its range will contract as climate changes and as we get warmer, hotter summers, warmer winters, and droughts."

Therefore, he said, it's a real imperative from many perspectives to mitigate climate change as fast as we can to . . . save the maple tree! [Exclamation point ours.]

"My life's work is to build the resilience of forests and to conserve them. I still think as gloom and doom as [the climate is], there's an inherent resilience to the forest of New England and the world. If we can just ramp down the stressors on forests, they will continue to function and provide all the benefits that they currently do," he said.

That means forests not being infringed on by development, fragmentation, or roads. He said that if we can effectively create policies and actions that reduce climate change, we can ultimately save syrup and maple products.

For the average consumer that means scrutinizing labels.

"Organic really means something when it comes to maple products," Finton said. "It means something for our own personal health, too. It means you're not using lead-based tubing or canisters for collection, or storage tanks that are not galvanized, so that we're not ingesting metals as we ingest the product. There are also forest management requirements to get those labels, including not tapping trees under ten inches in diameter and making sure that at least twenty-five percent of the species in the forest are not the same. You want a diverse forest because a diverse forest is a much more resilient forest and therefore much better at absorbing carbon and mitigating climate change.

"You know it would be easy to just create a monoculture of sugar maples and tap them. But that's moving away from being a functional forest that's effective for wildlife. A forest that is more of a monoculture, like a crop, is moving more toward a cornfield and away from being a forest. These organic requirements really help keep the forest as a diverse and resilient and functional entity. So, look at the label and be looking for the USDA organic label. Each state also has its own organic label.

THINK BEYOND PANCAKES

There are countless ways to get creative with maple syrup. We've included two recipes at the end of this chapter, but you can find tons of recipes online as well. Here are just a few ideas to get you started.

- a glaze for vegetables
- in ice cream
- for baked goods like cookies, muffins, and bread
- to coat nuts

Look for those, too. Searching for those labels and purchasing those products is something a consumer can do to have a direct impact on the climate."

He also pointed out that 75 percent of the forests in New England are owned by private landowners. And many of those are small patches of fifty acres or a hundred acres. "If we can incentivize and encourage those private landowners to keep their forests as forests, especially when·they need money to send their kid to college or what have you, instead of selling to a developer, that's really a win for conservation, a win for climate, and a win for the landowner," he said.

Maple, then, might just be the ultimate triple bottom line.

And the good news is there's already more interest in big-tree food products. Vermont is producing four times as much syrup as it did about a decade or so ago, according to industry statistics. This is keeping more forests intact. And conservationists are stepping in. The Nature Conservancy, which pretty much does what its name implies, bought a big tract of maple trees in Vermont from a paper company to preserve the land. Even so, commercial maple syrup makers are doing more with less.

Syrup producers explained that tree sap used to be hand-collected using buckets. Drill a hole in a tree, attach a pail to said tree, and wait for the sap to drip out. Relatively recent technology has sped things up, producers said. Vacuum pumps and tubes are attached to trees to better extract sap. The system can siphon twice as much sap as collecting by hand. That means makers are doing a heck of a lot more with less. The challenge for us consumers is to figure out how to eat and utilize more syrups like maple so that, despite the improvement in technologies, more trees will have to be planted.

Certainly, the demand for syrup can help suck up a lot of carbon. But there are more parts to the tree that we can use. The maple leaf, for instance, is being embraced by the cosmetics industry (leaf extract is apparently a wonder solution to preventing wrinkles), and the bark of maple trees is used for medicinal purposes as well as to smoke food. It's a cool thing to take a more holistic approach to using trees for all they offer without chopping them down.

While we're on the subject, there are even better ways to grow trees so they grow back bigger and stronger with more hunger for carbon. It's been the standard growing practice to plant tracts of the same species of tree. But as Andy Finton said, planting a mix of species of trees, rather than just one kind, can double the carbon-storing potential of that tract of forest.

EDIBLE LEAVES

We all know about eating leaves from small plants such as spinach, brussels sprouts, kale, cabbage, and the like. But certain leaves from trees that store carbon can be eaten, too. So, next time you make a salad, consider mixing in leaves from beech, birch, Chinese elm, fennel, mulberry, and others that can be plucked for their taste.

Which Bark Is Edible?

Survivalists often turn to the following trees listed in *Outdoor Life* for a taste of their barks:

- pine

- slippery elm

- black birch

- yellow birch

- red spruce

- black spruce

- balsam fir

- tamarack

Elm bark and pine bark are touted as especially good.

124

And to get the most carbon-storage buck from a tree, arborists say they should be planted where they are native species. In maple's case that means colder regions of the Northern Hemisphere. And maple isn't the only hardwood tree option. Birch, walnut, alder, sycamore, and several other species of trees have also been tapped for their sweet sap while leaving the tree intact to do its cool-food job.

Bark extracts are also a thing, especially pine bark extract. They are used as herbal supplements for use as an antioxidant, antimicrobial, and anti-inflammatory, among other purposes. We aren't suggesting that we all turn into Bear Grylls. But there is something to be said for using every part of a tree, especially if it means the tree can keep standing.

There are thousands of edible plants in the world. And while big hardwood trees capture the most carbon, and smaller trees less than that, and shrubs less than that, there are other ways we can keep food cool—how we cook, what we serve, and where we shop, chief among them. We cover that in our next section: "How to Eat Cool."

What Bird Lovers Choose Matters

The National Audubon Society allows its name to be used on certain food products that it has determined are grown or produced with birds in mind, such as coffee and maple syrup. This means that the producers of these products take into consideration bird habitats, stewarding land and forests in ways that benefit birds or capture more CO_2. Consumers who choose these products are supporting bird-friendly practices.

What You Can Do Today

- Only consume pure syrup products, not those made from artificial sweeteners.

- Buy maple products that carry the USDA Organic and Bird-Friendly Maple recognition.

- Use sugar crystals, creams, and extracts from big hardwood trees as healthy alternatives to other sweeteners.

- Try different colors of maple syrup. The darker, the stronger the flavor.

- Don't discard by color alone. Tree syrups keep for a long time even when their color changes.

- Look for products from Forest Stewardship Council (FSC) producers who pledge to protect and sustain the forests from which they get their products.

- If you live in or visit an area where maple trees grow, buy from a local producer to cut down on the energy and resulting pollution from transportation.

- Try sugar products from different hardwood trees such as hickory, butternut, and black walnut.

- Try derivative products. Ice creams, bread, and toppings can still create more demand for maple and other natural sweeteners that help protect the forests.

Gluten-Free Pancakes

INGREDIENTS
For the Pancakes:

¾ c. *RICE MILK*

4 tbsp. *VEGAN MARGARINE*, melted

2 extra-large *EGGS*, whites and yolks separated

1⅔ c. *GLUTEN-FREE FLOUR*

2½ tsp. *BAKING POWDER*

½ tsp. *SALT*

1 tsp. *BAKING SODA*

1 (15.25-oz.) can *PINEAPPLE TIDBITS*, juice reserved

1 tbsp. *SUPERFINE SUGAR*, to caramelize the pineapple

For the Butterscotch Sauce:

½ c. plus 2 tbsp. *PINEAPPLE JUICE*, from the can

¼ c. *LIGHT BROWN SUGAR*

2 tbsp. *VEGAN MARGARINE*, cut into cubes

2½ tbsp. *CORNSTARCH*

⅓ c. plus 1 tbsp. *COCONUT CREAM* (or your preferred vegan heavy cream substitute)

127

METHOD

To make the pancakes:

1 In a measuring cup, add the rice milk, margarine, and egg yolks. In a large mixing bowl, add the flour, sugar, and baking powder. In a second large bowl, add the egg whites.

2 Whisk together the ingredients in the measuring cup, then mix it into the flour mixture. Whisk the egg whites until fluffy, then gently fold them into the pancake batter with a spatula.

3 Heat a medium nonstick frying pan over low heat. Divide the pineapple tidbits into 12 batches and sprinkle each with superfine sugar. Put one batch into the pan, sugar side down. Let them caramelize for 30 seconds.

4 Use a ladle to pour ½ of the pancake batter over the pineapple to create an even, round layer. Cook for 3–4 minutes until the batter has stopped bubbling. Flip over the pancake with a spatula and cook the other side for another 2–3 minutes. Repeat the process with the rest of the batter to make 12 pancakes.

To make the sauce:

5 In a small saucepan, add the pineapple juice and sugar. Heat the juice over medium-low heat until the sugar has melted.

6 Bring the sauce to a boil. Add the margarine and whisk it in for 10 minutes over medium-high heat until the sauce turns a light caramel color. Turn down the heat and sift the cornstarch into the sauce. Whisk in the cornstarch and continue cooking for another 3–4 minutes, until thickened.

7 Remove the pan from the stovetop. Whisk in the cream until smooth and glossy.

8 Serve 3 pancakes per person, with a generous drizzle of butterscotch sauce.

SERVES 4 | PREP TIME: 5 MINUTES | COOKING TIME: 15 MINUTES
Recipe courtesy of Vegetarian Society

Maple and Chili Glazed Sweetcorn

INGREDIENTS

4 whole fresh **CORN ON THE COB,** husked

1 tsp. **MAPLE SYRUP**

CHILI SAUCE, such as sriracha, to taste

SALT and **PEPPER,** to taste

BUTTER or olive oil

METHOD

1 Place the corn into a pot of boiling water for 2 minutes, then drain. This will speed up the cooking process and help prevent the corn from drying out.

2 Place directly onto your barbecue. Cook for approximately 10 minutes, turning from time to time.

3 Mix the maple syrup and chili sauce together, then season with salt and pepper. Brush each cob with the mixture and cook for a few more minutes.

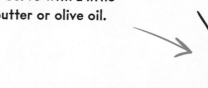

4 Serve with a little butter or olive oil.

131

Part Two

How to
Eat Cool

FARM TO TABLE

It's all about taste, not place. Cool seasons, you say? Indeed.

Farm-to-table cooking may seem like a simple formula for doing right by your health and the planet, but we learned that there is a lot more to it. Sure, it's easy to say, "Eat local." In many cases that is true. But not always. Which is why we ended up doing a whole chapter on the ins and outs and dos and don'ts of farm-to-table foods.

We were surprised to learn that sometimes the longer journey for certain foods at certain times of the year is actually better for us and the planet. And sometimes locally grown foods are laden with chemicals that can make climate change worse. To be sure, in general, the mantras of eating local and eating organic are good pieces of advice in the context of cool foods. But one of the big challenges is getting the right foods to market at the right time.

More than half of our fresh fruit and nearly a third of our fresh vegetables are imported from other

FAST FACT: It takes the average food item in the United States about fifteen hundred miles to get from the field in which it's grown or raised to the plate on which it's served.

countries. And those imports require both transportation and refrigeration. Carbon emissions from transporting food, or what are called "food miles," can be highly deceiving. It's all about the mode of transportation—truck, plane, train, or whatnot. The amount of food transported combined with the amount of carbon emissions used is what needs to be calculated on a net basis.

Obviously, heading out to your garden and picking a piece of fruit or a nut from a tree is one of the best options. Not all of us can do that. If we're to examine the most common ways we get our food (at the grocery store), then on a net basis, carbon footprints vary and, in many cases, surprisingly so. You might think that, for instance, importing food to the

United States from China would in all cases be the worst for the environment in terms of transportation pollution, but that isn't the case. Shipping food by sea is the most efficient way to transport it, followed by train, truck, and air. In fact, shipping anything by air is about seventy times more damaging to the planet, in terms of carbon emissions, compared to shipping something of the same weight by cargo ship. So flying fruit from Boston to Chicago (about a thousand miles) carries a much bigger carbon footprint than shipping that cargo by sea from China to California (nearly seven thousand miles).

This goes for animal products, too. Animal products carry the biggest carbon footprints of anything we eat, and even they have better and worse carbon footprints. For example, we learned lamb from New Zealand has a far lower carbon footprint than sheep from England, even for local English eaters and even taking into account the eleven-thousand-mile journey, because

136

THE 1950s FOOD REVOLUTION

Most Americans actually ate almost exclusively local foods until just after World War II, we learned. The advent of suburban living, interstate highways, processed foods, and the supermarket concept combined to make industrially produced foods easier for people to buy even if they were shipped from long distances. New cooling—refrigeration—and storage facilities also helped. The move away from local produce began, and, many would argue, taste suffered for it.

It may be hard to imagine, but refrigerators weren't widely available in homes until the 1950s. The ability to keep food frozen meant that it could last longer. And it also provided the makings for an entire new food category: TV dinners. These ready-made meals could be frozen and popped in the oven— something that we take for granted today. Interestingly, the first of these frozen dinners were repurposed airline meals.

Refrigeration technology combined with the dawn of TV advertising gave rise to huge sales of these frozen dinners. A radically different way of eating took hold of America, and high-volume food manufacturing quickly followed. This necessitated fertilizers and preservatives. Industrial farming had to proliferate to keep up with demand and a booming population's appetite. Local and family farms were replaced.

Until the turn of the twentieth century, people working on farms composed nearly half the US population. By 1970, that number fell to less than 5 percent of the population; by 2000, it fell to less than 2 percent. Farm workers have been replaced by industrial processes and technology. Family-run farms are among the tiny minority now—and so is the food from them.

Kiwi sheep are largely raised on farms run by hydroelectric power.

Still, many people have become "locavores" to help promote the benefits of all things local. And that isn't a bad thing; it shows the desire to understand where food comes from, and that is a great path for learning how food affects climate.

The biggest contributors to any food's carbon footprint are how it is grown, transported, and stored. According to TerraPass, which sells carbon offsets so people and organizations can balance out their carbon emissions, 83 percent of food CO_2 emissions comes from production, which mainly consists of growing and storing food. TerraPass notes that storing food uses a lot of electricity and therefore in many cases creates more CO_2 emissions than transporting that same amount of food.

A study was done to figure out if refrigerating food was worth the environmental cost. After all, without refrigeration, food spoils. That creates food waste, and food waste, as we've learned, results in environmental pollution of different sorts. But even with all that food loss—given that we Americans lose about half our food to waste—in North America greenhouse

Carbon Offsets

Carbon offsets are a way to balance the emissions you produce by purchasing negative emissions credits. These credits come in different forms such as trees that are planted or soil that is made healthier to draw down and keep more carbon in the ground. The amount of carbon that is kept stored by these methods is calculated. Then the amount of CO_2 you produce is matched against these totals. You purchase the difference so you can "balance out" your own carbon footprint.

What's in Season Now?

Here's a quick rundown of some of the more common cool foods listed by their seasons:

Winter

Chestnuts	Lemons	Tangerines
Grapefruits	Oranges	

Spring

Apricots	Pineapples	Artichokes
Avocados	Strawberries	Fava Beans
Mangoes		

Summer

Blackberries	Peaches	Tomatoes
Blueberries	Plums	Watermelons
Nectarines	Raspberries	Green Beans

Fall

Apples	Pears	Pumpkins
Cranberries	Pomegranates	Sweet Potatoes
Figs	Quinces	
Grapes	Butternut Squash	

FARMERS' MARKETS ARE BOOMING

One in five Americans consumes locally grown food at least twice a week. And that has translated into a surge in farmers' markets. The US counts about eight thousand of them now. There were fewer than two thousand farmers' markets a decade ago.

....

gas emissions due to refrigeration are worse; about 10 percent greater, in fact. Fresh food is therefore the best way to avoid carbon emissions. In the big picture, freshness keeps things cooler.

Often our best choice for fresh goods is a farmers' market because these markets almost universally sell locally grown products, much of which are organic.

But when we're not shopping at a farmers' market, how do we know where our food comes from? Country of origin labels (COOL) on foods can help. We see these most prominently on such things as bananas and avocados. Look closer and you'll likely find them on other foods, too. We did. And while you are paying attention, a good seasonal food guide can help keep things fresh and tasty throughout the year. We discovered that local grocery stores often provide these guides on their websites, showcasing what's fresh and in season depending on your geographic location. Otherwise, it takes just a few clicks online to figure out what's being harvested and when.

You, like us, probably can taste the difference when you eat foods that are grown locally and in season. But do you ever wonder how taste works? We did. Here is how medical professionals describe the biology of it all: The bumps on your tongue contain taste buds, or tiny hairs, that send messages

"Ironically, I never went to a farmers' market until I lived in New York City. And even then, I went for the experience, not so much the food. The market became a place to meet friends and walk around. Sure, there was fresh food and odd jams and strange cheeses. But it was more about the activity than the eating. Certainly, it wasn't about getting weekly groceries. In New York, groceries were a meal-by-meal shop.

"When I lived in London, it was a similar thing. Borough Market was my destination for interacting with friends and vendors. Borough Market now is a true foodie destination, filled with pop-up eateries, restaurants, and all kinds of food experiences—not just local farm fare.

"Los Angeles is different. Even though there are far more organic and specialty food shops in LA, the farmers' markets offer a connection to what many call the Breadbasket of America; California is the biggest agricultural producer in the United States. The fresh taste comes through. It's the farm-to-table food for me now that is the center of attention."

141

to the brain, which then translates the messages as sour or salty or sweet and the like. When you're young, you have about ten thousand taste buds. As you age, your taste buds get depleted down to about half of what they were when you were a kid. Taste buds get replaced about every two weeks, and they combine with scent, or the chemicals that are released up your nose when you chew. Taste is the combined message that your brain translates into all the nuanced words we have for flavors in our vocabulary.

The science and subjectivity of taste are fascinating to explore. But can environmental benefits be linked to taste? Particular types of grains, vegetables, fruits, and even animal breeds are disappearing from the food chain, as we've discovered. Foods that are easier to grow and those mass produced by industrial agriculture often stack supermarket shelves because they are cheaper and more convenient for buyers to get their hands on. In many cases, that means taste suffers. And taste is linked to freshness. In turn, freshness is linked to what's grown locally. Yet how do we laypeople who don't have the luxury of a sophisticated culinary education know what can taste better? Without getting too out there and ontological about it, how do we know what we don't know?

Try a fresh-off-the-vine tomato and compare it to one wrapped in plastic that has been sitting on the supermarket shelf for a while. Bite into a ripe apple that you've picked from a tree. Or pop a grape into your mouth at just the right season. Taste explodes. But if you've never done any of those things, you can only imagine the differences.

Taste education is something that chefs are advocating. Famed chef Alice Waters, who is largely credited as a founder of the farm-to-table movement and a pioneer in promoting the benefits of organic food, promotes the Slow Food goal to "prevent the disappearance of local food cultures and traditions, counteract the rise of fast life and combat people's dwindling interest in the food they eat." Over a long evening meal at her latest restaurant, Lulu, at the Hammer Museum in Los Angeles, Waters walked us through her journey to becoming such an iconic culinary figure.

Known for her restaurant Chez Panisse's role in championing the farm-to-table movement, Waters's many accolades and accomplishments include a Michelin Star, a James Beard Foundation Award for Lifetime Achievement, a Global Environmental Citizen Award, and a National Humanities Medal. She is also credited with inspiring the White House organic vegetable garden and establishing the Edible Schoolyard Project, the Yale Sustainable Food Program, and the Rome Sustainable Food Project at the American Academy, among others.

"It's all about the senses," she said. "More people need to pay attention to them to find their way, their passion."

That may seem like vague California advice, but it's deep and it's meaningful, and it's what led Waters down the path of advocacy. "I was in France, and I was served a bowl of wild strawberries. I put one in my mouth and there was this explosion. I had never tasted anything like them. And I just said, 'Where did this come from?' And that is what really started my

THE COOL FOOD TRIFECTA: LOCAL, SEASONAL & ORGANIC

Sourcing foods from local farms reduces carbon emissions by about 5 percent per food item. By paying attention to which foods are in season, that number can be pushed to 10 percent or more—again, by staying local and organic.

culinary exploration," she explained.

Next came bread. "I just saw all these people standing in line to get bread. And I said, why are they standing in line? So, I stood there with them. And then I got this hot champ [potato bread], and then I said, I know why they're standing there. And every day when I went past the markets supposedly to go to school, I saw people in line for food—not because they had to, because they wanted to," she recalled.

Then she had an awakening: "I came back a year later, and I said, 'I want to eat like the French.' It was really as simple as that. But I couldn't find that taste. And then I had this crazy idea. I said to my parents, 'Maybe we need to just go open a restaurant and we'll find that type of food. It's probably available for restaurants, not stores.'"

But that wasn't so much the case either. She ended up chasing taste and looking for freshness the only way she knew how, which was to visit local farms. The ones that had the freshest taste happened to be organic. So, lesson one was the exceedingly good taste that organically grown food brought. Later, that elevated to the enhanced flavors that regenerative soil brings to food. And that lesson came from her father.

She said, "He drove around to all these farms to help me, and one day he came back and said, 'Taste this, it's ten times better than anyone else's.' And it was. It was companion planting. The farmer was Bob Cannard, and he has been my farmer for years and years." Companion planting is the practice of growing different yet complementary plant species together for the mutual benefit of warding off disease and insects. In short, it makes them grow better by making them more resilient.

That was another lesson: a direct connection to farmers and the local community.

Now let's back up a step. Waters briefly taught at a Montessori school

144

after college. And that method of teaching, which encourages independent thought and creative choices, informed her connection to nature and how we think about food, she said. To empower others, she pioneered the Edible Schoolyard so kids could forge their own connections to nature and food—another way for them to express themselves.

It's always been about freedom of expression: Her connection to better food, emboldening her desire for different tastes. Her connection to local farmers, supporting their important role in the food system. Her work in the schools, fostering children's education. And her food policy advocacy, giving us all a chance for better nutrition. Indeed, in her mind, she said, she's always been an activist.

Her current push for reform is with the USDA school lunch program, encouraging more locally grown organic fruit and vegetables to be incorporated into students' diets. "We could connect schools with their local farms. Think of all the money that could go toward supporting the local economy," she said. (We'll take a closer look at school lunches in chapter ten.)

But first, we all must learn to become our own best food advocates. The way to do that—and to understand the difference between the traditional, processed food system and an alternative system that supports local, organic foods—is to do what Waters originally did: go to farmers' markets and taste the difference.

Sensorially educating oneself takes effort. It involves researching, studying, and visiting markets and farms to learn about taste and freshness. It means learning which restaurants serve fresh foods and understanding how chefs prepare them. And it means putting freshness at the center of your weekly grocery shopping experience.

A simpler way, we learned, is to look for certain labels on food. The choices aren't always perfect because

Organic Labels

Food that is labeled . . .

→ • "100% organic" must contain only organically produced ingredients.

→ • "Organic" must contain at least 95 percent organically produced ingredients.

→ • "Made with Organic" on a product (like soup) must contain at least 70 percent organic ingredients.

food labels aren't always perfect. Yet by paying more attention to labels, we can all better identify cool foods.

There aren't restrictions around labels such as "sustainably harvested," so the best we can do is to look for the certified organic label from the United States Department of Agriculture. The USDA regulates what is deemed organic. The agency specifies how organic agricultural products are grown, processed, and handled. Produce can be called organic if no synthetic fertilizers or pesticides have been applied to the soil from which the crop is grown in the previous three years, the USDA says in its literature explaining the guidelines. When it comes to processing, organically processed foods cannot contain artificial preservatives, colors, or flavors. (Although, there are some exceptions, such as yogurt enzymes, pectin from fruit preserves, and baking soda.)

What's so bad about pesticides and synthetic fertilizers? Pesticides are defined as toxic substances designed to prevent, destroy, repel, or mitigate pests and help food grow. They can cause serious health problems in humans, according to medical research.

Synthetic fertilizers, meanwhile, are chemicals that can artificially help plants grow. Plants need nitrogen, phosphorus, and potassium to grow, and fertilizers stimulate this growth, according to the science. Still, synthetic fertilizers are made by burning fossil fuels. One study shows that nitrogen uses so much natural gas and coal that it can account for more than half of the total energy used in commercial agriculture. Depending on the location, oil can account for as much as 75 percent of the energy used. Obviously, that sends the carbon footprint of many commercially grown, nonorganic crops through the roof and is one reason why agriculture adds so much to carbon emissions and global temperature rise. Hence the reason why organic labels are

GMOs

Genetically modified organisms (GMOs) are "organisms (i.e., plants, animals, or microorganisms) in which the genetic material (DNA) has been altered in a way that does not occur naturally by mating and/or natural recombination," according to the World Health Organization. For the most part, that means artificially altering the way seeds or livestock are grown.

important to look for on the foods we buy. Unfortunately, some labels are very misleading.

"Anybody and their uncle can say they're green right?" Michael Oshman noted. He's the CEO of the Green Restaurant Association, a Boston-based nonprofit organization that, according to their website, encourages "restaurants to green their operations

Misleading Labels

According to the nonprofit **FOOD AND WATER WATCH**, an organization whose research we found particularly insightful, a few misleading labels to look for are . . .

Free Range

This label only applies to poultry meat, not eggs. And it doesn't apply to cattle or hogs or any other animals.

The only thing this label really explains is whether artificial colors, flavors, or preservatives were added. It does not denote if antibiotics or hormones were injected into foods.

Natural — Naturally Raised

148

Fresh

The only applicable food to which "fresh" officially applies is poultry. It means poultry meat was not cooled below twenty-six degrees Fahrenheit. Poultry is considered frozen when it's been stored at zero degrees.

Pasture Raised

This only means that animals were outside for some time—but doesn't indicate how much time nor what type of environment the "pasture" really is.

Some other labels are hard to even figure out. Genetically modified food labels fall into this category. The fact that a food was grown or raised with any kind of genetic modification technically must be disclosed. But how this disclosure appears can be misleading. Products can simply include the information on a barcode or list a toll-free number to call for more information.

The Green Restaurant Association (GRA) Certification System

The GRA certification system takes the guesswork out of choosing a restaurant for diners who want to eat at a sustainable establishment. Thousands of restaurants across the country display the certification decal to indicate they have earned certification. Certified Green Restaurants® have had their sustainability practices verified against transparent, science-based certification standards based on over thirty years of implementation and research. Anyone can go to dinegreen.com and find Certified Green Restaurants® nearby.

using transparent, science-based certification standards." Over the course of several conversations, and at least one attempt at breakfast, we learned exactly what diners really care about when it comes to sustainability.

"Consumers want their experiences to be real. If I'm going to bother buying an organic orange at the supermarket, it better be organic. Otherwise, why go out of my way to go to that supermarket? Why might I be paying more money for that? And why would I be wasting my mental capacity to search for this one versus that one, unless it's doing something really good for the world? Same with restaurants," Oshman said. "There's a sense of transparency. And I think this is a key piece of not only finding your favorite restaurant but also knowing what it means to be green and choosing that restaurant versus some other one."

Something like 70 percent of the time, diners will choose a green restaurant over a traditional (nongreen) restaurant. It's a huge differentiator.

So, what does it mean to be green?

"There are seven environmental categories—energy, water, waste, disposables, chemicals, food, and building. That pretty much encompasses everything that can happen in a restaurant. What am I eating? Where did it come from? Is it going to the garbage or to the compost? Is the plate being cleaned with green chemicals? What about pest control? Or are the tables made from sustainable materials? Is the takeout in reusable disposables that are properly disposable? Is the restaurant bringing enough green lighting? What type of energy is used for cooking? So, we encompass everything so the consumer doesn't have to," Oshman said. And many don't want to. The best green restaurants are the ones where you don't notice anything different. It's what's behind the scenes that matters.

The GRA certifies everything from fine-dining establishments to airport cafés to school cafeterias. And it turns out that no restaurant is perfect.

"James Cameron's wife, Suzy Cameron, has a school up in Malibu. Their cafeteria has gotten the most green points of any restaurant—period. They're vegan. They're solar. They hit all the marks on the food, on the energy. They're doing fantastic. And even they have room for improvement," he said.

It creates a hive. Oshman says a green rating means a restaurant must carry certain items, like vegan items, organic items, energy-efficient items, or recycled paper products. All those products necessitate a different type of vendor. "And it behooves those vendors to start selling to other restaurants in the area. It's not economically advantageous to sell that one product to one place. So, I would say our impact is much greater than greening each restaurant. And we

151

human beings, we see what's in front of us. And if we see a lot of activity in that one neighborhood, we're more likely to go there. It grabs attention and it has this multiplier effect that creates impact," Oshman said.

What's more, other restaurant owners decide to go green. "So now, even if a restaurant owner hadn't thought about or cared about being green, now they do because they want the business," Oshman said.

In turn, dining experiences get better. Green restaurants attract more passionate employees, Oshman said. "They're going to feel better about working at this place. They're going to have more longevity, more loyalty, more honesty, and diners get better customer service.

"So really what the consumer is getting when they see that certification is the same thing as when they see the organic certification: they might not know exactly what it means, but they know it's good and it's better than the other thing. So back to where we started, they'll say, 'I'm going to go get that organic orange.' I think for most consumers, that's the story," he said.

Choosing which items to eat and when, figuring out which labels to abide by, deciding whether to eat local, and choosing among food groups can be daunting, we know. Thankfully, more restaurants are doing their bit for us. The number of restaurants choosing to go green and become more sustainable is growing, along with the number of people who prefer organics, we found.

There are something like six hundred thousand restaurants in the United States. Only a small percent of them are sustainable. Think about how much of an impact could be had if all or even the majority swapped in cool foods for even one dish on their menus.

As mentioned, the Green Restaurant Association has thousands of members—and it's growing—and is an easy one-stop shop to find a local restaurant that adheres to sustainability standards. Its standards include water efficiency, recycling, reducing waste, serving sustainable food, minding energy use, and educating patrons on environmental practices.

One of the bigger environmental issues that certified green restaurants try to address, we're told, is food waste. And it, like farm-to-table foods, is such a big and important subject in the cool food effort that we decided to give it its own chapter. You can read that next.

What You Can Do Today

- Check the origins of foods and educate yourself about what grows on farms near you.

- Remember, local is cool—but not always. Check for which foods are in season and where.

- Look for the USDA certified organic label. Foods that carry the certification have to abide by stricter guidelines for artificial fertilizer and pesticide use.

- Be wary of misleading marketing labels like "fresh," "free range," "pasture raised," "natural," and "naturally raised."

- Know that foods containing genetically modified organisms (GMOs) can be sly about how they display information.

- Try to dine at a sustainable restaurant. The Green Restaurant Association has a long list of restaurants around the country to check out.

Baked Apples with Raisins

INGREDIENTS

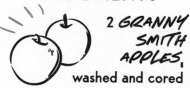

2 *GRANNY SMITH APPLES*, washed and cored

Pinch of *CINNAMON*

3 tbsp. *RAISINS*

2 tsp. *HONEY*

1 tbsp. unsalted *BUTTER*

METHOD

1 Preheat the oven to 350°F.

2 In a small bowl, combine the raisins with honey and cinnamon, then stuff each apple with the mixture.

3 Top each apple with a little butter.

4 Stand apples on a lined baking sheet and bake for about 45 minutes until softened.

5 Serve in bowls.

Recipe courtesy of Vegetarian Society

Avocado and Lime Salad

INGREDIENTS

1 head crisp lettuce, such as *ROMAINE*, finely shredded

1½ c. roughly chopped *WATERCRESS*

½ small *ENGLISH CUCUMBER*, diced

1 small *RED BELL PEPPER*, diced

1 bunch *GREEN ONIONS*, sliced

2 *AVOCADOS*, pitted, skin removed, and diced

2 rings of *PINEAPPLE* (canned), cut into chunks

3 *LIMES*, juice only

1 clove *GARLIC*, crushed

3 tbsp. *OLIVE OIL*

SALT and freshly ground *BLACK PEPPER* to taste

Handful fresh *CILANTRO*, roughly chopped

METHOD

1 Mix the shredded lettuce and watercress together and scatter over a serving platter.

2 In a bowl, mix the cucumber, pepper, green onions, avocados, and pineapple together and reserve.

3 Whisk the lime juice, garlic, olive oil, salt, and pepper together to make a dressing. Add to the chopped vegetable mixture and mix well. Spoon over the lettuce and watercress on the platter and scatter the cilantro over the top.

4 Chill the salad for about 30 minutes before serving.

157

FOOD WASTE

Leftovers? Boy, are there lots of ideas. And expiration dates? Maybe not.

While we're all about erasing our carbon footprints by what we put in our mouths, we learned that it's just as important, if not more important, to mind what doesn't make it into our stomachs. There's a lot we can do to cut down on food waste and, in turn, prevent tons of greenhouse gases from entering the atmosphere, warming temperatures, and causing climate havoc.

We learned why methane is such a big problem for the United States: we toss more food than any other country. The research shows that in the US we waste about a third of the food we have at home by overshopping and underconsuming. And at restaurants, we also typically leave anywhere from 30 to 40 percent on the plate when it's taken away.

This sends tons to landfills, where food is the most abundant item among all the trash. That all translates into enormous amounts of methane gas escaping into

FAST FACT: The total amount of methane gas emissions from food waste in the US per year totals as much pollution as that produced from the exhaust of thirty-seven million cars on the road.

Methane

In addition to being released from a food's dying cells when it decomposes, methane comes out of exhaust pipes, leaks from wastewater treatment facilities, and other industrial processes. It's also produced naturally from wetlands and animal digestion.

....

the air when the food is left to rot. Methane, remember, is the second most abundant greenhouse gas, after carbon dioxide, that leads to global temperature rise and climate change. Clearly, to help food keep our planet cool, we need to reduce food waste.

That said, most of us Americans think that we do a good job cleaning our plates without wasting food; more than two out of every three of us in the US believe that we throw out less food than our neighbors, according to studies of food habits we read. But our beliefs, according to the numbers, don't add up. We need to face the facts: we all need to cut back on food waste.

The most common types of food that are spared from our digestive tracts only to find their way to the tops of the heaps at landfills are bread, milk, coffee grounds, apples, potatoes, and pasta. Seems as though we can stand to be more discriminating with how and what we consume, right?

For inspiration on how to do this, we turned to Douglas McMaster, a trailblazer of the zero-waste movement. He owns and is the executive chef of the famed Silo restaurant, as well as the host of *Zero Waste Cooking School*.

Back in 2014, McMaster was burned out on cooking at some of the world's best restaurants, including the

FAST FACT:
On average, each person in the United States tosses away about a pound of food per day.

Fat Duck and Noma. He said he was thinking, "*I don't know what to believe in anymore. I don't know what to do.*

"That's when I met this artist. He was an absolute genius who said to me, 'Could you not have a bin?' And it was an unusual timing because he had just built a building out of waste materials. It was a restaurant that was entirely made from waste. And then I just kind of fell in love with his work." The artist he was referencing is Joost Bakker, a founding member of the zero-waste movement, and the suggestion of having a kitchen without any trash can was revolutionary for McMaster.

"From that moment, I had this sense of fulfillment, this sense of purpose." And so, McMaster's own zero-waste odyssey began. "Since then, that's my whole life," he said.

His zero-waste restaurant Silo was born in the seaside town of Brighton in the UK and moved to East London's übercool Hackney Wick section in 2019. It's a spectacular space. And nearly

FAST FACT:
Half the food supplied to restaurants never even makes it into your mouth. At home, we waste nearly as much.

everything with which Silo was built has been recycled. The reception desk was even made from the excess wood left over from the restaurant's construction. The handsome design features white walls, and the menu is projected against one of them (to save on paper menus). The floor is carbon-negative cork. The tabletops and bar are made from recycled packaging. Plates are upcycled plastic bags. There is a sophisticated design element and luxurious quality to everything. Perhaps, and maybe especially because McMaster thought he might become a fine artist like his father, he has a refined eye.

In any event, the food is, well, the main course in the display of zero waste.

Seated at a table overlooking the canal that runs by the industrial complex atop which Silo resides, McMaster explained, "You're going to have a dessert tonight. It's an ice cream sandwich. The ice cream is made from buttermilk. We're churning butter for your bread and butter. Heritage grain from the farm is used to make the sourdough. The by-products from that first plate of food, the bran from the bread, become a wafer for your ice cream sandwich. And then the remains of the bread itself, we make a syrup from that. So, it's closing the loop from three surplus products from the first course."

The full-circle approach takes a lot of creativity. The outside leaves of cabbage that typically go to waste are made into a dish using fermented egg whites, for example. Egg whites also often go to waste. ("There's only so much meringue you can make," he said.) And portions matter, too: there is just the right amount of food on each plate.

The staff educates diners about each serving. It's not pretentious. You actually feel good while fine dining and knowing that you're being mindful. And that's the whole point—conveyance.

"That mindfulness can be instrumental in how the shift in society will hopefully make the food system better. I'm absolutely big on what mindfulness can do," he said.

The takeaway on minding waste is infectious and is something that can be carried home. "There's all these basic tips like composting. If you can't have it at your home, then connect to a local composting system. Or proper recycling. Understanding how your local recycling system works. Or freezing foods. Or batch cooking. There's all these little things. They add up. They matter," McMaster said. (For more tips, tutorials, and recipes, check out his *Zero Waste Cooking School* on YouTube or his book, *Silo: The Zero Waste Blueprint*.)

His ultimate mission is to hold out a culinary movement defined by principles of respect for the planet: "Waste is a symptom of an unsustainable food system, or any system, for that matter. The more waste there is, the more unsustainable our system is. So, it's kind of a marker . . . A truly sustainable food system in the world would mean balance to the inputs and our relationship with natural resources. That includes our emissions. It's all about creating harmony," McMaster said.

In the back room of the restaurant, behind closed doors, he points out the garbage bin. It's smaller than what many people have in their homes—and Silo serves hundreds of meals a week. And guess what? Those remains will get composted.

No bin.

▲ ▲ ▲ ▲ ▲ ▲ ▲ ▲ ▲

Make no mistake, sticking to a slimmed-down food program doesn't translate into a forced diet program; it simply better matches how much food you should get versus what you actually eat. And wasting less

comes with a bonus: $1,500. That's how much the average family of four could save in a year if they planned meals properly.

Obviously, our appetites vary, and sometimes we change our minds about the type of food we feel like eating. Which leaves food fated for the bin. If you find yourself with an abundance of perfectly edible food, food banks are a great way to donate to those in need. They accept untouched food. And for home gardeners with excess produce, AmpleHarvest is a great organization to turn to. According to their website, they leverage technology so that home and community gardeners can "share their surplus harvests with nearby food pantries instead of letting them go to waste." Food pantries register online and report what foods they need. Home gardener registrants respond and fill the request. It's a super simple online matching system.

"Look at the food recovery hierarchy," Dr. Jean Buzby, the US

Food-Saving
TIPS

To help us all do a better job lessening our food footprint, the USDA put together a program that helps us save food while we shop, cook, and store it for later use. Storing different foods the right way helps them stay fresh longer and prevents them from spoiling and being discarded. Here are some of their tips:

STORAGE

Put most vegetables into the high-humidity drawer in your fridge, including leafy greens, carrots, cucumbers, and broccoli.

Most fruits ought to go in the low-humidity drawer.

Store the following fruit away from other produce: bananas, apples, pears, stone fruits, and avocados. They release ethylene gas that makes other produce exposed to it spoil faster.

Keep the following separate as well in cool dry places: potatoes, eggplants, winter squash, onions, and garlic.

Wait to wash things like: berries, cherries, and grapes until you are ready to eat them to prevent mold.

164

Food-Saving TIPS

SHOPPING

Plan meals weekly—not daily, and certainly not monthly. This can also save money and time.

Keep a running list of meals and their ingredients that you've already eaten. You're more likely to consume meals that you've already enjoyed.

Make a list of what to buy based on what you'll eat at home, taking into account how often you'll eat out, as well as which meals you can make from leftovers.

Do an inventory to see what you really need versus what you already have on hand.

Remember that quantity matters, especially with vegetables where an item such as lettuce can be good for two meals or more.

Note that "saving" can come at a price: "buy one, get one free" deals only save money if you use all the food before it spoils.

Purchase "imperfect foods" to save money. Imperfect foods are those that don't look as good but are otherwise fine to eat.

IN THE REFRIGERATOR, LOCATION MATTERS

Don't place your milk and other highly perishable items in the refrigerator door; the warmer air to which it is exposed every time the door swings open increases the chance of spoilage.

Department of Agriculture's Food Loss and Waste liaison, suggested. "The first thing is to not create waste through lots of ways in the first place. But then the second tier is if you do have excess food—that's wholesome—you want to get it to those in need through food banks and so forth. And if that can't be done, then the next best alternative is to turn it into animal feed. If it's not so wholesome [processed food] and that's

"We don't waste food in the Downey household. There are too many mouths to feed and not all of them are human. We have Kunekune pigs, goats, alpacas, bunnies, mini horses, and a feline to serve. I'm happy to say that our compost takes a more direct route into fertilizer than most. Pigs, especially our matriarch Lady Bug, are great at producing the stuff. We've all benefited from seeing up close the full cycle of growing, eating, and using the waste to grow again. Hate to cut it off here, but I've gotta get Lady Bug her homegrown salad for lunch."

not possible, then there's a category of industrial uses like upcycling it to other value-added products. And then there's a tier for composting. And if you just can't get any valuable soil amendements, then the very bottom of the pyramid is landfilling and incineration," Buzby explained from her living room in Virginia as she wrangled one of her dogs.

Buzby said there is no single silver bullet to food waste; its effect is far and wide, touching nearly all aspects of our lives. "We're talking about our humanity, really. It affects the climate, our use of resources. It touches the amount of finite arable land we have, fresh water, and food security. The scale of this is so massive with the growing world population. This is really a big deal," she said.

But there's hope.

She said there are several things we can do in the first place to reduce waste. As discussed, we can be more mindful about our shopping and know what we already have in our cabinets. That includes perishables, the most important category in the food-waste arena. "Buy what's perishable and you know you're going to use in the next few days," Buzby advised. "There's other simple things to get in the habit of: mark the date and contents of your leftovers. Put them in transparent canteen containers so you can see at a glance what you have. You could even have a leftover night, like every Tuesday. Having a plan is the big deal. And, of course, there's composting. I think a lot of people don't realize how much they really toss," she said.

Besides the garbage itself, waste can add up to thousands of dollars per year, and for businesses, even more. She said the World Resources Institute found in a research study that businesses can achieve a fourteen-to-one return on their food inventory simply by purchasing smarter. Incentives clearly abound.

Consumer labeling is a big part of her focus. She collaborates with the Food

167

Know Your Food Dates

Often-misunderstood labels are "sell by," "use by," and "best by" dates. These are not food safety dates. They are supposed to be used for flavor, peak quality, and inventory management purposes. Throwing away food based on these dates creates even more waste. The USDA admits this and says misunderstanding adds to the waste problem. The real way to know if food has spoiled is to examine it. Spoiled foods will smell, taste, or look different than they should.

and Drug Administration (FDA) as well as the Environmental Protection Agency (EPA) to raise awareness and promote the fact that expiration dates on food labels mostly only apply to food quality, not safety. In terms of safety, she says, infant formula is the only exception.

Buzby has been working on the food-waste issue since 2002 and sees perhaps the biggest chances for reductions now. "Even though this issue is here to stay, I've seen it get more and more attention, both domestically and internationally. And I think it's such a big issue now that it's really resonating. So, I'm hoping it will take off like recycling—it just becomes part of our everyday life and we practice just doing the right thing," she said.

Facilitating the effort is the United Nations Sustainable Development Goal to halve food waste around the world, as well as that initiative among federal agencies in the US to halve losses by 2030. To help, the USDA, EPA, and FDA have joined forces for the International Day of Awareness of Food Loss and Waste (September 29). Information is on their respective websites.

"It's going to take all of us to really reduce food loss. This is a problem from the farm all the way up to the kitchen or a consumer's table. And we all have things that we can do," Buzby said.

It's a top-down approach.

Still, let's say you've done a good job planning, storing, utilizing, and donating most of your food, yet the remainder has spoiled or just can't be eaten. You can still prevent it from ending up in a landfill, where it does the planet harm, by composting, as Buzby suggested. Compost is a natural fertilizer made of organic materials such as food and yard-trimming waste.

Composting can keep a lot of waste from making its way to a landfill, which, by the way, likely involves transportation by a garbage truck of some sort that burns fuel and emits pollution, adding even more to the environmental cost of food waste.

If planning, storing, and composting all seem overwhelming, yet you'd still like to lessen your food-waste load, try a meal kit program. We learned that meal kits are superefficient.

WHY MEAL KITS ARE COOL

Many meal kit programs have a much lower carbon footprint versus buying groceries at the store—as much as 33 percent—because of all the efficiencies meal kit companies can achieve by planning at the corporate level.

Meal kit delivery services do all the planning, shopping, and portioning for you. You get to choose what you want to eat and have your meals prepared or ready for you to make at home. We found that there are many planet-friendly food choices that are sustainably packaged. And many of the food companies behind the programs and services pledge to offset 100 percent of their carbon emissions. (We'll explore meal kits more in chapter thirteen.)

▲ ▲ ▲ ▲ ▲ ▲ ▲ ▲ ▲

How to Compost

OUTDOORS

1 Find a dry, shady spot for your compost pile.

2 Add brown and green materials in equal amounts. Brown materials are things like dead leaves, branches, and twigs. Green materials are fruits, vegetables, and coffee grounds.

3 Moisten the lot.

4 You can cover it with a tarp or keep it exposed, ensuring that grass and the like are on top with food waste underneath.

INDOORS

The EPA is mindful that not everyone can have an outdoor compost bin: "If you do not have space for an outdoor compost pile, you can compost materials indoors using a special type of bin, which you can buy at a local hardware store, gardening supplies store, or make yourself." Place your waste and materials in the special bin. In about two weeks, it can be used as fertilizer.

Note that there are certain items that you *shouldn't* compost, such as walnuts, dairy products, oils, meat, and fish. These aren't good for the soil's health.

170

The food recovery hierarchy doesn't just apply to us consumers. As Buzby pointed out, businesses are major culprits of food waste even though it's in their best financial interest to reduce what they throw away. Companies should be able to tackle inefficiencies and buying challenges better than we can at home because they employ professionals to manage their supply orders. Businesses can also follow a lot of the same guidelines and tips outlined in this chapter. And they can sign on to the USDA's food champion program to show their support for the initiative.

As we mentioned earlier, about 50 percent of the food served at

> **FAST FACT:**
> The average full-service restaurant wastes seventy-five thousand pounds of food per year, adding up to losses of more than $160 billion annually across the whole industry.

> **FAST FACT:**
> In 1996 Congress passed the Bill Emerson Good Samaritan Act, protecting restaurant owners and other commercial operators from liability stemming from food donations.

restaurants is wasted, and the lion's share of that waste comes from us not eating everything we order. Because of labor costs, excess food—even food that didn't make it onto plates—is often cheaper to toss than use for ingredients in another meal. That is likely the main reason why restaurants only donate approximately 2 percent of the extra food they have purchased. The rest, we found out, ends up in the garbage. Additionally, many restaurant operators are confused about what they can and cannot donate; fears of liability abound.

Technology is changing food waste ratios for the better. A bit of online research revealed a slew of web-based

DO YOU KNOW YOUR STATE'S FOOD POLICY?

A group called ReFED, which is all about rethinking food waste, created an online state-by-state food policy finder where you can look up which laws are on the books and may apply to you or your business. The URL is

PolicyFinder.ReFED.org

Check it out.

applications that allow restaurants to notify shelters and nonprofit organizations of their excess food so the food can be picked up and donated fresh. And artificial intelligence is apparently helping to better match supply and demand.

Even the food that has been tossed can find a home other than a landfill. We were turned on to a rising number of start-up companies that have begun collecting food waste and turning it into biochar, which is a form of charcoal that can be spread onto the soil to make it healthier. Organic farmers see value in buying biochar for their croplands, and as a result, food can go full circle—from pasture to plate and back again.

As we consumers have begun asking for more planet-friendly foods, state regulators are following the mindset out the back door . . . where the trash is. From what we've seen and read, new waste regulations will be good for us, and good for the restaurant industry, too. Regulations are a necessary and long-awaited wake-up call to the food-waste problem that is contributing to climate change.

We learned that five states—California, Massachusetts, Connecticut, Rhode Island, and Vermont—have passed laws to try to keep food out of landfills. And many more states have bills that address food waste in some way, from offering tax incentives for

172

FOOD WASTE: PAST AND FUTURE

We came across a fascinating digital exhibit put on by Utah State University about the history of food waste. It showed and discussed how Native Americans utilized nearly every part of the animals they killed, leaving little to no waste. The various uses—fur as clothing, castor as bait, fat as candles, and more—were picked up by early explorers, fur trappers, or "mountain men." This was during the early 1800s in the West.

When Mormons settled in rural Utah, they, in turn, learned these skills from the mountain men. Food security became an important edict. Members of the Mormon church began to formalize methods for food waste, including donating extra food and storing supplies for future use, as well as helping those in need. These concepts spread. In fact, the church mandates that all members keep enough food stored for months at a time for themselves and for other members who may be less prepared.

Food waste has been an issue for the general population of the United States since its founding, and even more since industrialization. The USDA was partially created because of the food waste issue. During World War I, the agency began a series of promotional campaigns to prevent waste. The USU exhibit discussed this and the campaigns for "Meatless Tuesdays" and "Wheatless Wednesdays." The campaigns featured those famous call-to-action posters of the era. They entwined food savings with patriotism. "Food is ammunition,"

CONTINUED →

173

read one poster. "Don't waste it." The Dust Bowl necessitated food relief programs for farmers. World War II prompted more federal campaigns to stop food waste. Post-WWII saw the invention of fertilizers and pesticides that made it easier to grow food—and waste it. So much so that garbage disposals were introduced to make it easier to discard food.

food donations to date labeling. California's law was enacted in 2022 and requires people to put their food waste into a special green bin, much like the blue bins used for recycling. The green bins don't go to landfills. Instead, they are transported to facilities that can convert the waste into natural gas and be used as a renewable energy source, or into natural fertilizers for farmers and gardeners, like that biochar we just mentioned. Residents and businesses that don't comply with the law face fines of up to $500 a day. The law's goal, as written, is to reduce food waste in the state by 75 percent, along with saving all the methane created.

While food waste may seem like a local issue, we learned that it's truly an international ordeal. The United Nations is tackling it through its Sustainable Development Goals program, which is bringing attention to the issue. "Think, Eat, Save" is how the UN is promoting its plan to reduce our "foodprint." The goal, according to the UN's literature, is to halve food loss through better production, handling, storage, processing—and our consumption. Its Food Waste Index measures tons of wasted food per capita around the world.

We know that food is increasingly becoming the center of attention for the planet's health. And, sure, the better and cooler the food that we eat, the more it will help put a stop to climate change. But food waste needs to be managed in parallel. So much of the food-waste discussion seems abstract, out of mind—when

174

we toss something, it's gone, away. It becomes someone else's problem. The problem, though, doesn't really go away; it just becomes a problem for all of us.

Let's face it—it's too easy to let the business of life get in the way of doing what is best for us. And this doesn't just apply to how easy it is to waste food. In the next chapter, we'll look at the quick and convenient meals that so many of us turn to when time is short—and how we can make them cooler.

What You Can Do Today

- Try not to overorder at restaurants.
- Be mindful of how much food you buy at the store, especially bread, milk, coffee, apples, potatoes, and pasta.
- Plan your meals weekly.
- Follow the tips on pages 164 and 165 on how to store different foods to keep them longer.
- Compost inedible fruits, vegetables, coffee grounds, and other scraps whenever you can—just not meats, seafood, walnuts, or other foods that corrupt the soil.
- Donate untouched food to a food bank.
- If you grow your own fruits or vegetables, donate the surplus to food pantries via matching services like AmpleHarvest.org.
- Plan meals using leftovers.
- Try a meal kit service; they rescue waste and carbon emissions.
- Remember "sell by" labels are only guidance; they are not steadfast spoilage dates. The only true way to figure out if food has spoiled is to examine it yourself.

Recipe courtesy of Vegetarian Society

Vegan Banana Choc Chip Muffins

INGREDIENTS

1 c. WHOLE-WHEAT FLOUR

1/2 c. plus 2 tbsp. OLD-FASHIONED ROLLED OATS

1 tsp. CINNAMON

1 tsp. BAKING POWDER

1/2 tsp. BAKING SODA

1/2 tsp. SALT

2/3 c. ALMOND MILK or plant milk of choice

4 "FLAX EGGS"
(1 flax egg = 1 tbsp. ground linseed/flaxseed, ground and mixed with 1 tbsp. water. Set aside for 10 minutes to thicken before use.)

2 tsp. CIDER VINEGAR

1/3 c. MAPLE or AGAVE SYRUP

3/4 c. melted COCONUT OIL

1 tsp. VANILLA EXTRACT

3 small ripe BANANAS, mashed

1/2 c. SEMI-SWEET CHOCOLATE CHIPS

METHOD

1 Preheat the oven to 350°F and line a 12-hole muffin pan with baking cups.

2 In a large bowl, mix the flour, oats, cinnamon, baking powder, baking soda, and salt.

3 In a slightly smaller bowl, mix together the plant milk, flax eggs, vinegar, syrup, coconut oil, and vanilla extract. Mix until well combined and there are very few flax egg lumps.

4 Add the milk mixture to the flour bowl and mix with a wooden spoon until just combined. Add in the mashed banana and chocolate chips. Mix again.

5 Divide the mixture among the 12 baking cups.

6 Bake in the preheated oven for 20–25 minutes. Gently insert a knife to check if they are cooked. If the knife comes out clean of batter, they are done. You may see a little melted chocolate on the knife—this is fine. Check for uncooked batter.

7 Transfer to a wire rack to cool.

Recipe courtesy of Vegetarian Society

Lentil and Tomato Dahl with Wholemeal Roti Bread

INGREDIENTS

1 tbsp. EXTRA-VIRGIN OLIVE OIL

1 small ONION, finely chopped

1 clove GARLIC, finely minced

1-inch piece fresh GINGER, peeled and finely minced

1 CARROT, peeled and diced into small pieces

1 small POTATO, peeled and diced into small pieces

1 tsp. ground CUMIN

⅓ c. RED LENTILS, washed

2½ c. reduced-sodium VEGETABLE BROTH

1 (14-oz.) can STRAINED TOMATOES

8 oz. canned GARBANZO BEANS, drained

1 tbsp. LEMON JUICE

Pinch of GROUND BLACK PEPPER

1 WHOLE-WHEAT ROTI (or tortilla)

METHOD

1 Heat the oil in a large saucepan. Add the onion, garlic, and ginger and fry gently for 5 minutes.

2 Add the carrot, potato, cumin, lentils, broth, and strained tomatoes to the pan. Bring to a boil, then turn the heat down to a simmer. Cover the pan and cook for 20 minutes, stirring occasionally.

3 Add the garbanzo beans and more water, if needed, and cook for a further 20 minutes, continuing to stir from time to time.

4 Ladle the dahl into bowls and top with a squeeze of lemon juice and a little black pepper.

179

5 Serve with whole-wheat roti (or other flatbread, such as tortillas).

FAST FOOD

A quick way to help
fix the climate?
We'll shake to that. With some fries.

Most of us eat at home more than we eat away from home, according to the various studies that we read. And while it's obviously important to be climate conscious when we shop and cook, it's also important to be climate minded when we eat out. The places we most frequent for food when we aren't cooking are fast-food joints, and there are lots of climate issues connected to fast food—never mind health considerations.

What we order sends a message. And fast-food restaurants seem to have received our memos about climate change and health by taking steps to offer more meals that are nutritious and that do right by the climate. We learned that the biggest fast-food chains in the world are adopting more environmentally friendly practices and offering more items on their menus that are planet focused. This can help slow time on the ticking-clock problem that food presents to the planet's health.

FAST FACT:
One out of three of us Americans eats at a fast-food restaurant every day, and around 80 percent of American families order fast food at least once a week.

181

Restaurant Types

There are 11 types of restaurants:

1. **Fine dining**
2. **Casual dining**
3. **Contemporary casual**
4. **Family style**
5. **Fast casual**
   (a.k.a. healthy fast food)
6. **Fast food**
7. **Café**
8. **Buffet**
9. **Food truck/concession**
10. **Pop-up**
11. **Ghost restaurant**
    (delivery only)

Tip: Contemporary-casual restaurants are more prone to follow eco-friendly protocols and serve healthier food.

McDonald's advertises that it has served billions and billions of meals. (It reportedly stopped keeping count in 1994.) And those meals have come at an enormous environmental cost. But the opposite can happen, too. For instance, we learned that 630,000 animals' lives were spared in 2021 because fast-food restaurants incorporated more plant-based meals into their menus. Considering all the savings from raising those animals, the environmental benefits significantly reduced the world's carbon footprint.

COW BURPS

The 220 pounds of methane that a cow belches out per year is nearly twenty-five times worse for the climate than if it were carbon dioxide gas. And that's just what comes out of a cow's mouth, never mind all the greenhouse gases associated with making what goes in.

FAST FACT:
The average American's consumption of beef alone over the course of a year produces the same amount of greenhouse gases as driving a car for 1,800 miles.

According to the data, livestock takes up about 80 percent of agricultural land yet only produces about 20 percent of our calories. At the same time, raising livestock produces the most global greenhouse emissions in the agricultural food sector, and the agricultural sector accounts for more than 10 percent of all greenhouse gas emissions here in the US. We know that the feed, water, and energy it takes for an animal to grow and then be processed into meat strain natural resources and pollute the planet from the animal's birth to its death. We found out that most steers and heifers are butchered before they are three years old. But that's still three years' worth of resources and pollution from millions of heads of cattle.

Clearly, reducing meat helps the climate. Switching a burger for salad even once a week can save tons of carbon pollution from entering the atmosphere. If everyone in the US did this, it would be like stopping the pollution from twelve million cars. But fast food isn't all about meat (whether beef, poultry, or fish). Fast-food restaurants serve a lot of vegetables, too, though vegetables total a small percentage of sales.

Of course, more salads on the menu is the clear winner when it comes to cool food, but eating a salad isn't the same experience as eating a burger. Which is where plant-based options come into the picture.

Plant-based foods are largely made with grains, pulses, or other vegetables. They look and taste like the traditional animal-based items for which they are meant to substitute. We discovered that this doesn't necessarily mean they are vegan because there may be additives that come from animals. (Vegan food has zero ingredients that come from animals.)

183

PROS AND CONS OF VEGGIE MEATS

Plant-based meats are as much as 90 percent better for the planet than animal meat. Although, it should be noted, this doesn't mean they are healthier for you. You may be depriving your body of important nutrients such as vitamin B, certain fats, and calcium.

The most common plants used as a meat replacement are soy, peas, beans, mushrooms, mung beans, or seitan (which is actually wheat gluten). These are made to look and taste like different meat products. Pigments make the mash red or brown or marbled. Nuts and seeds help bind the food together. Then there are the flavorings. Burgers, sausages, nuggets, hot dogs, deli meats, and ground beef are what we see most as meat replacements at the grocery store. Innovative dishes can fool you into thinking that you are eating animal meat when you're not. Plant-based steaks now even come marbled so they have the look and texture of real beef.

The promise plant-based meals hold for the planet may be awesome, but so is the potential for fast-food restaurants' profits. We found out that it can be cheaper and faster to make plant-based meals than anything made from traditional animal meat if enough supply can be had to drive down costs. Spread meat replacement efforts across the more than two hundred thousand fast-food spots in the US alone, and there is a seriously formidable agent of change that could turn things climate positive quickly.

"We need to be able to reverse global warming," said Kaj Török, the chief

FAST FACT:
Nearly half of all Americans began eating more plant-based food during the pandemic.

184

WHY IS IT CALLED A HAMBURGER ANYWAY?

Legend has it that in the nineteenth century, German sailors got the idea of eating raw, shredded beef from Russia, where it was served in the Baltic provinces. Germany and Russia were early trading partners. A chef in Hamburg, Germany, apparently decided to cook the meat— and the hamburger was born. The burger idea eventually made its way across the Atlantic Ocean and was first featured in the United States at the Saint Louis World's Fair in 1904.

Even though the hamburger may have been born in Germany, it has been adopted as quintessentially American. Fifty billion hamburgers are served annually in America alone. A meal of a burger, milkshake, and fries has become part of a kind of USA nostalgia associated with small-town America, diners, and simpler times. Its popularity was forged on the back of the fast-food industry, symbolizing, according to *The Atlantic* magazine, America's "exceptionalism and industriousness." Not only did it come of age at the same time as industrialization, but it was also, and arguably still is, a shining example of how we make fast food better than anywhere else on the planet—even if the planet itself suffers for it.

CORPORATE CLIMATE STRATEGIES

Ceres, a nonprofit organization in Boston, combed through food companies' corporate reports in a study and found that few of them have climate-friendly strategies in place—or at least disclose that they do. Investors and eaters are one and the same, and Ceres says more food companies should do a better job of climate stewardship.

(You can learn more about Ceres's Food Emissions 50 initiative and which food companies are the most climate friendly at Ceres.org.)

sustainability officer at MAX Burgers in Sweden. MAX used to be called MAX Hamburger but dropped the "ham" several years ago to emphasize its focus on promoting greener burger options. It's now a climate-neutral restaurant chain and is considered a pioneer in the climate-positive movement, embracing sustainability and pushing the envelope to inspire other fast-food chains to become more climate friendly. It's working. Both Burger King and McDonald's have stepped up their environmental menus' offerings and sustainability approaches in their competition with MAX. That's certainly a competitive spirit that bodes well for customers and the climate alike.

"We're actually transforming beyond our own industry. And I'm so happy

FAST FACT:
Vegan meals are, on average, 40 percent cheaper than a similar meal of meat or fish.

for that. I can imagine a day where companies or governments are capturing more carbon than we emit," Török said.

Still, it isn't, in his view, enough simply to reduce emissions.

"We must be climate positive now," he said. "I hear this saying all the time: 'The most important thing we can do right now is to reduce our emissions.' Well, we already have the speed. It's not enough to just reduce the speed a little bit. We should stop, and we should go back, and we should find better routes. This is not the route we're going for. We need a new paradigm. It's too late for climate neutral. It's too late to just reduce emissions. We need to have this kind of setting where we restore some of the things we have already lost. We need to be able to reverse global warming."

To do that, MAX focuses on serving more climate-positive food.

"Of course, we have things like double-sided menus, reduced packaging on takeaway, and do eco/EV driving. But that's all the symbolic stuff that really doesn't mean anything when it comes to climate change. The big things are the food. It's 85 percent of our carbon footprint. When you look at the whole value chain—and most companies don't look at the whole value chain—what we know now is that if you choose the fresh plant burger, instead of the traditional cheese-and-bacon-with-beef burger, you can reduce your carbon footprint by 87 percent. So, the most important thing we can do is to inspire our guests to choose burgers with low carbon footprint," Török said.

Inspiration, in this case, is synonymous with sales. "It's not enough to have it on the menu, but how is it sold?" he asked rhetorically.

"We communicate it for those who like really good-tasting burgers: 'Here are some new options.' What we learned is that the major thing when it comes to food is it's about the culture, actually. What is your taste culture? Do you like a barbecue burger? What kind of protein? What do you want with it?

187

Mix around with that. Lots of options instead of, 'Are you a vegan?' 'No, I'm not a vegan.' 'Okay. Sorry.' We're finding different ways of putting it on the menu all the time and in our advertising and our commercials," he said.

And yet that is *still* not enough. Coaxing people through the door only gets you so far in terms of sales, he said. Taste matters most, driving return customers and boosting word-of-mouth marketing and the like.

"The most important thing we can do right now to reduce our carbon emissions is to make sure that burgers

FAST FOOD'S COOL PLANS

Burger King has set a target for going 50 percent meat-free by 2030. And McDonald's, KFC, Taco Bell, and Pizza Hut have also committed to reducing their climate footprints to help keep the world cooler.

with a low climate impact taste at least as good as those with a high-end impact. So, taste is everything. It's everything for our guests, everything for us, everything for our sales, and as it turns out, everything for the future of the planet," he said.

The reason this matters globally is that the fast-food industry is highly competitive. Practices that produce higher sales and customer loyalty are adopted by other fast-food chains. Which is why choosing a low-carbon-impact meal, even halfway around the world, still affects us all—climate positively.

How restaurants achieve their climate-saving efforts vary, we found, but most are doing two things: offering plant-based alternatives to meat and auditing just how many greenhouse gas emissions they produce.

Animal care may not have been much of a key concern for fast-food restaurants in the past because so much of the meat they historically have served has been processed meat. Processed meat

188

is chemically preserved, salted, smoked, fermented, and treated in other ways to improve its taste and how long it lasts on the shelf before spoiling. It's anything but cool. And when you look at the sheer amount of that meat that is eaten, it isn't difficult to see that change is needed.

Four times as much meat is produced globally now versus fifty years ago, and along with it, more livestock that trample the ground. The United Nations estimates that about a quarter of all the land on Earth is used to raise animals for us to eat. Moreover, it says, one-third of all farmland is used to grow food for those animals. The more land that is occupied or developed as a feed crop resource, the warmer the planet.

We learned that McDonald's is looking at ways to reduce greenhouse gases at the source of its animal supply chain. It's experimenting and analyzing cattle's impact on the climate through different grazing techniques. How and what cows eat is a key driver of climate change. When too many animals graze on the same patch of land, it destroys the soil. Degraded soil stores less carbon, as we've learned, and that leads to increased global temperature rise. The methane released from feeding animals (especially cows) lesser-quality food also makes climate change worse.

By feeding cattle better-quality food that reduces methane emissions and allowing cattle to roam, McDonald's says that—along with its other efforts—it can reduce its corporate climate footprint by more than a third by the end of the 2020s. That plan alone could prevent 150 million tons of carbon emissions from entering the atmosphere, which is pretty cool.

In addition to figuring out different ways to reduce the impact on the climate by growing crops and raising

....

livestock differently, McDonald's and other restaurants are also experimenting with advanced food technologies to lessen their carbon footprints.

Cultivated meat is one thing they're eyeing. Animal stem cells are grown in a lab and served as meat. This eliminates the raising and slaughtering of animals yet provides the similar taste and protein as live animals. The benefit for the environment is big: no feed or water or soil degradation. A laboratory-grown meat's carbon footprint—if the lab utilizes renewable energy sources—can be nearly 20 percent lower for chicken, more than 50 percent lower for pork, and more than 90 percent lower for beef. And when it comes to price, cultivators claim they can produce meat for less than the price per pound of conventional animal production.

Given that processed foods, cell-based foods, and plant-based proteins are human inventions made to taste like natural flavors, the importance of incorporating our senses into taste and flavor can only be expected to grow. Does that veggie burger really taste like a hamburger made from beef? Do those chicken nuggets have any chicken flavor? What about that fake bacon? But it isn't just taste and texture that can fool our brains into thinking we are eating something other than what's in our mouths. How something smells and looks, as well as other externalities, can enhance or detract from the flavor.

We learned a lot about all this from Charles Spence, a food psychologist—

technically, experimental psychologist—at Oxford University. His research focuses on how our brains process information from our senses—smell, taste, sight, hearing, and touch—and how a better understanding of the human mind can lead to better design of foods, products, and environments in the future.

For example, Spence speaks of things such as "sonic seasoning": how different music changes the taste of foods. Or the color of plates that create "visual deliciousness."

"What's on your tongue is the least interesting bit of taste and flavor," he said. Instead, multisensory perception affects food's appeal in deeper and more interesting ways. This is what Spence calls "the perfect meal."

"The perfect meal is sort of an idealized concept. It's something that probably most people can understand. Over the last five or ten years, what was your perfect meal? We all have one, maybe a few. It's different for each and every one of us. For some, it might be a meal they had somewhere in the middle of a country they had never been to before. For others, it might be a picnic in the middle of a forest. Or it could have been a meal by the seaside. Now, there are things you can extract from analyzing great meal experiences, then you can sort of feed them back to people," he said.

For our interview, Spence was in the cloud forest in the mountains outside of Bogotá, Colombia, where he spends months at a time every year getting more in touch with the sights and sounds of nature. He said that lighting, temperatures, scents of forests or seas, and the sounds of nature can encourage better moods. Moods inform taste. In short, Spence studies memories. Which is a longer version of what our brains do anyway when we eat.

"Most of the time we don't really taste. We always, before we put anything in our mouths, we always make a prediction of what it's going to be. Our brain predicts energy content, fat content, and then pays attention accordingly. We always kind of live in the world of our sensory predictions, no exception to that. Our brain predicts a flavor using sight, maybe sound, maybe touch, maybe the occasional nasal sniff. Then your brain says, 'Okay, I think that's energy dense. I think I like it, blah, blah, blah.' Then you taste it. And somewhere during the tasting, you might check, 'Is it what I expected it was going to be?' If what you actually taste is what you predicted beforehand, then you live in the world of your flavor predictions, not in the world of flavor experience. And that's why vision can have such a dramatic role because that's the cue that is most informative," he explained.

Now augment or alter those sensory experiences. That's what Spence does to enhance flavors or give people a completely new food experience. He talks of one example where diners are served jellyfish: They put on headsets, and the sound of crunches is played. When people eat the jellyfish, they think it tastes like Pringles potato chips. He devised another similar experience

with insects to make them appealing to eat. Or he can repel. He said, "We served two hundred diners a duck dish in a London restaurant. But before the duck dish came out, you heard the final moments of the duck's life. We were trying to nudge people away [from eating it], but in a playful, humorous way. 'If you don't want to know what happened to the animal you're eating, why are you eating it?' kind of thing."

Restaurant chains use similar sensory levers, even if we don't realize it. Hard Rock Cafe and Planet Hollywood play really loud and fast music in their bars because that increases drink sales by 30 percent, Spence said. Fast-food restaurants like Subway, KFC, and Cinnabon try to position their locations at the bottom of stairs—the olfactory

FAST FACT:
The colors red and yellow can make you feel hungry, which is why they are used so much by fast-food chains.

sense beckons you right in. McDonald's has bright lights and colors so people eat fast and leave.

Sensory experiences can even be used to give people multiple tastes in their mouths at the same time or flavors that trick their brains. "Can we make food that's interesting or inspiring, magical, frightening, or shocking? A lot of our work in the last year has been working with magicians to find out if you could eat magic or a magical flavor. Can we make people shiver or relax? You know, there are even foods that can change flavor as you're reading about them," Spence said.

Using his work, maybe we can trick ourselves into eating for a better world.

▲ ▲ ▲ ▲ ▲ ▲ ▲ ▲ ▲ ▲

Seeking out restaurants that have a corporate conscience about how the food they serve is grown or raised, as well as avoiding processed meat, are ways that we eaters can support fast-food efforts that are climate friendly. Soon we may even be able to look for cell-based proteins and other "future foods" on menus (we get into this later in the book). More choices will give more voice to the cool food movement and allow planet-friendly options to thrive.

Fast-food restaurants are using different methods of advertising to let us know about the plant-based alternatives they have on offer. For instance, the chain restaurant Panera Bread highlights the Cool Food Meal badge on its menus and explains that the badge is used to designate that a menu item has low food-related greenhouse gas emissions.

The badge is used by other food outlets, too, so that's something to look for. But it's tricky, we learned. Seeking out cool food items requires a bit of investigation; it's less about being "sold on" than "bought" out of our own consumer want. Most plant-based options are merely indicated as vegan or vegetarian (v) on menus. Being "planet friendly" or "cool" isn't held out very

193

Chipotle

In the United States, Chipotle Mexican Grill is often referred to as one of the most planet-friendly restaurants in the fast-food category. They make environmental transparency part of their customer experience and track how much climate impact is achieved through every order. In their corporate reports, they hold themselves accountable for better/worse achievements and explain how they can do better. Still, we shouldn't have to read corporate reports to make our dinner choices. We're thinking that more restaurants ought to brandish their climate friendliness to customers rather than burying that information in corporate filings.

much in promotions. Which is curious given the seeming rise in demand for vegan and plant-based foods.

A more helpful designation would be details about the carbon count of ingredients, places of origin, and whether the food has been grown organically. In other words, a carbon label, much like the calorie counts that are mandated on many restaurant menus and menu boards throughout the country, would be far more helpful to us climate-conscious consumers rather than just indicating whether something is vegan.

CALORIE COST

The US Food and Drug Administration (FDA) in 2018 began mandating that calorie counts be listed on menus of restaurants that have twenty or more locations. In doing so, it cited health data that showed eating a single meal away from home each week translates into an extra two pounds of weight gain per year.

Even in the fast-food world, we don't have to go vegan to help save the planet. Pair a burger (organic, wild pasture, grass fed) with a cool food side dish, such as sweet potato fries, and the entire meal can become climate positive. The opportunity for this to be replicated over and over millions of times in the fast-food industry could create an impact that is global and enormous. This also puts the climate power of takeout food and everyday meals into everyday people's hands.

Volume is how the food business can truly turn the climate positive. Take MAX Burgers. It sells more hamburgers in Sweden than McDonald's, and it has been on a climate mission since 2008, when it says that it became the first restaurant in the world to claim a "climate-positive" approach. Every year since, it has published the most comprehensive climate analysis in the restaurant industry. But its impact can only be realized by more sales.

We read how MAX makes their burgers climate positive: First, they measure and calculate greenhouse gas emissions—from the farm to customers' plates. This includes transportation (to and from a restaurant) and waste. It also reduces emissions throughout its operations by taking into account things like heating, waste, and packaging. Finally, it offsets 110 percent of the emissions that it produces by planting trees in Uganda, Mexico, and Nicaragua. An independent accounting firm reviews all its methods to certify its standards. MAX takes the guesswork out of going climate positive; it does the hard work for us.

Industry experts say the future of fast food around the world is with plant-based offerings and menus like

FAST FACT:
Fast-food restaurants came along with the advent of America's highways in the 1950s, when people began driving long distances more and wanted food on the go.

"Eating at MAX Burgers in Stockholm, where the company is headquartered, was quite a cool experience, especially as I was afforded a taste test of different plant-based menu items—burger, chicken nuggets, grilled cheese—and the climate-positive aspect of everything that I was chewing was explained to me by the sustainable product development team who joined me for lunch. Veggie burgers and nuggets made from soy; a strawberry milkshake made from coconuts. Even the carton and paper packaging were detailed for their compostable possibilities.

"Serving thousands of meals per day means there can be a big footprint to step in the right direction. And MAX Burgers is indeed walking the planet-friendly walk that it talks so much about. Yet it's the taste that strikes most. Burgers don't taste like cardboard or leave an unpleasant film in the mouth. (There is thought put into that.) There is a striving for freshness. ("Can you taste the strawberries, not the syrup, the actual strawberries?" I was asked.) The goal is to make the plant-based options just as tasty as the items they are meant to replace, if not more so.

"On a leafy terrace in the hip Medborgarplatsen area of Södermalm—Stockholm's Williamsburg, I am told—the fact that I was eating fast food was lost. The plate tasted like good food. Which is really the whole point. 'Well, it's all pointless if it doesn't taste good,' said MAX's Török. 'People shouldn't be questioning what they are eating; it should taste the same.'"

MAX's. A healthier and more sustainable supply chain that caters to increased demand will drive down prices and encourage more environmentally responsible practices. But that all rests on increased customer demand. Which is another way of saying it's what we order at the takeout counter and the drive-through that matters most and that can change how chain restaurants operate, including what they offer. A cooler, happier meal, perhaps?

The good news is there's a new generation on the horizon that may be poised to change the world as we know it for the better. We'll see how in our next chapter.

What You Can Do Today

- **Order a salad rather than a beef burger at fast-food restaurants.**
- **Choose plant-based meats instead of animal meat and eat vegan.**
- **Avoid processed meats.**
- **Pair a burger with more planet-friendly sides (sweet potato fries, for example) to offset the carbon emissions from a fast-food meal.**
- **Be on the lookout for the Cool Food Meal badge. It means the restaurant is concerned about climate change and is taking steps to mitigate its carbon footprint on the planet.**
- **For specific food items, check out carbon labels. They act like a calorie counter for the planet, and the less carbon the better to keep things cool.**
- **Seek out climate-conscious corporations using keywords such as "climate-positive food" coupled with a brand's name.**

RECIPE

Quick Kidney Bean Burgers

INGREDIENTS

I clove GARLIC, CRUSHED

I (16-oz.) can KIDNEY BEANS, drained and rinsed

2 TOMATOES, finely chopped

1 tbsp. SOY SAUCE

1 c. BREADCRUMBS

⅓ c. SEMOLINA FLOUR

I tbsp. VEGETABLE OIL

I tbsp. LEMON JUICE

2 heaped tsp. DRIED MIXED HERBS

METHOD

1 Mix together the beans, tomatoes, garlic, and herbs in a large bowl.

2 Add the breadcrumbs and semolina. Mix well.

3 Add soy sauce and lemon juice. If necessary, add a tablespoon of water to increase moisture (but don't be tempted to add any more!).

4 Shape into burgers. You can freeze the burgers to cook another time at this step if you like.

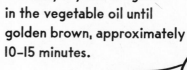

5 Gently fry the burgers in the vegetable oil until golden brown, approximately 10–15 minutes.

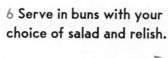

6 Serve in buns with your choice of salad and relish.

199

NOTE: This recipe is meant as a fun and playful experiment for the senses. Audio headphones are suggested to play a track that emits a crunching sound (available via popular audio streaming platforms). That is what is meant by "crispy"—not the actual texture of the jellyfish. Close your eyes, listen, and eat. What are you eating? If you didn't see the dish, could you guess?

Crispy Jellyfish

INGREDIENTS

I lb. *JELLYFISH*, shredded and soaked in cold water overnight (you can buy jellyfish at Asian supermarkets)

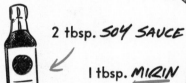

¼ c. *WHITE SUGAR*

2 tbsp. *SOY SAUCE*

I tbsp. *MIRIN*

3 tbsp. *RICE VINEGAR*

3 tbsp. *SESAME OIL*

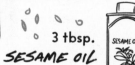

I tbsp. *CHILI OIL*

3 tbsp. *CHILI SAUCE* (gochujang)

1¾ tsp. *SESAME SEEDS*

METHOD

I With the exception of the jellyfish, place all of the ingredients in a bowl, mix together, and set aside.

2 In a separate bowl, place the jellyfish and add the marinade one spoon at a time, massaging it in by hand.

3 Once all the mix has been incorporated, leave the jellyfish to marinate for an hour, at which point it is ready to serve.

201

Nukazuke Cucumber Gazpacho

INGREDIENTS

8 c. *RICE BRAN*

⅓ c. *SEA SALT*
(or kosher salt)

½ c. *BEER*

3 tbsp. *WATER*

1 small
*WHOLE DRIED
CHILI PEPPER*

2 tbsp. *KONBU*
(Saccharina japonica)

1 clove *GARLIC*

4 large
CUCUMBERS
(sliced lengthwise
into quarters)

¾ c. fresh
*CUCUMBER
JUICE*

METHOD

1 Toast the rice bran over a low heat (use a dry pan). Once toasted and cooled, add the sea salt and beer, and mix by hand or using a wooden spoon. Add the water a little at a time until the bran has the texture of "wet sand." Add the chili (large slices), konbu (cut into strips), and garlic (large slices). This mixture is called a "Nukadoko" (i.e. pickling bed).

2 To prepare the mixture for pickling, it must first be left for a week with a few "test" pieces of cucumber (or other similar vegetables). Each day the nukadoko must be agitated by hand in order to grow both lactic bacteria and wild yeast in good balance. After a week, remove the cucumber. The nukadoko base is now ready to ferment.

3 Take three large cucumbers (quartered lengthwise) and rub with coarse salt (to increase their surface area), then quickly rinse and bury in the nukadoko. Leave overnight, then remove the cucumber and rinse any excess bran mix off with cold water.

4 Juice the pickled cucumbers in a blender. This juice may be excessively sour (as a result of pickling) and salty, so there may be a need to balance out the taste/flavor with fresh cucumber juice. Serve as a cold cucumber gazpacho with Crispy Jellyfish.

20ㅈ

SCHOOL LUNCH

**Cool kids are going vegan.
Let's serve them lunch.**

There are more than seventy-three million kids under the age of eighteen in the United States. That's nearly a quarter of the population. (A government census put the US population at 332 million in 2022.) Considering that the vast majority of these promising, curious, nutty, and often excited individuals are students, what they eat makes a huge difference for the planet. That's why school lunches are insanely impactful on the climate change that affects us all. We found that a few simple switches of food items can result in a massive reversal of climate ramifications. For example, swapping just one student meal per week for a more planet-friendly serving could save five million tons of carbon dioxide from polluting the sky. That's as much carbon as more than six million acres of forest store in a year.

Neat fact, right? Nearly two thousand schools apparently think so, too. That's how many we found

FAST FACTS:
The median cost of school lunch in the United States is $3.00 for middle grade and high school students. For elementary school kids, it's $2.75. Breakfast is $1.80 for high schoolers, $1.75 for those in middle school, and $1.73 for elementary school children.

that have reported opting to make this kind of climate-friendly meal swap. They are part of a growing network of school systems communicating with one another to make mass change. The Oakland Unified School District in California disclosed that by switching to plant-centered diets, it saves money—veggies are less expensive than meats—as well as other natural resources such as water. The district says it has cut its water use by 6 percent, which saves even more money—tens of thousands of dollars per school year.

Of course, less meat greatly reduces carbon emissions, too—as we know, it takes a lot of carbon-polluting energy to raise animals. Cool foods that keep carbon stored rather than used and ending up in places it shouldn't be—freewheeling around in the sky, for example, and latching onto the sun's rays—could make even more of a difference.

We read a report published online by an environmental organization with a welcoming name, Friends of the Earth, that said if every school district in the country eliminated animal foods from their menus, it would slash 700 million kilograms of carbon emissions from being released into the atmosphere, equivalent to 150,000 cars driving 1.6 billion miles. This would also be like installing solar on about one hundred thousand homes and taking them off a fossil-fuel-sourced energy grid.

So vegan school lunches aren't such a bad start to help fix the climate. And green vegetables are famously packed with vitamins and minerals important to children's growth and health. Changing what kids eat is tricky, though. As any parent knows, there's a balance between serving kids foods that are nutritious and healthy and what tastes good.

We learned something interesting about why some kids dislike their veggies so much. Scientists recently discovered that broccoli, brussels sprouts, and cauliflower contain enzymes that release putrid odors when mixed with certain people's saliva, especially found in kids'

mouths. Children are also more sensitive to bitter tastes because they have about twice as many taste buds as adults. A conundrum is whether the saliva-enzyme mix changes as we age, or whether we just adapt and get used to different flavors. And if you're an adult and still hate your veggies, there may be a scientific reason for that, too: a gene identified as TAS2R38. It regulates bitterness sensitivity and is an early alert signal for the human body that something in your mouth may be toxic. It can mistake the bitterness of, say, broccoli for poison. You're apt to spit it out.

So, what may seem like a simple suggested switch to eating more vegetables comes with its challenges. But they're challenges worth tackling.

In January 2022, Eric Adams took office as the 110th mayor of New York City, and one of his first acts in office was to implement a vegan lunch program for America's largest school district, serving vegan lunches on Fridays. He said

"I can't take any credit for making my kids' school lunches, but Susan and I try to look after everything they eat. Most kids have coaches for one activity or another. My youngest son has a Little League coach, a tennis coach, and a basketball coach, but food coach is the cap Susan and I find ourselves wearing most often these days. We practice a lot of mindfulness in our household, and we try to integrate that mindfulness with our kids when it comes to food. However, I do have a bad habit of midnight snacking, which is not a food-coaching technique I want to pass on to them."

WHY SCHOOL LUNCH COMES WITH MILK

School lunch programs in the United States date back to the nineteenth century, and even earlier in Europe. US government programs were largely begun during the Great Depression, when people couldn't afford to feed their families. This also came around the same time when the government began subsidizing agriculture to assist farmers. Milk (from cows) became an indelible part of this assistance and is the reason why, many believe, the dairy industry is so powerfully entwined with the school lunch program—and why plant-based foods and drinks find it challenging to be added onto school lunch menus.

Agricultural support and school lunch programs came together in 1946 when the National School Lunch Act was passed into law. It laid out how meals should be served and included basic nutrition requirements: pints of milk; meats, cheeses, and fish; dry peas and beans; peanut butter; and bread were all listed as main meal portions. Over the following decades, lunch programs and nutrition requirements evolved and eventually became informed by the 1977 McGovern Report (which we mentioned way back in chapter four) that suggested the US populace eat healthier foods. The report discussed which foods specifically should be part of a national American diet, encouraging less fatty, sugary, and processed foods to be served. It also took aim at obesity and undernourishment of schoolchildren. Those tenets also form the basis for today's USDA national diet program.

the timing was right, not only in terms of his tenure—an early act to signify the importance of plant-based food—but also in terms of acceptance by city residents. Adams himself is a vegan.

"When I look over the last few years, we are at a place where many people thought it was not possible," he said, drinking a self-made green smoothie out of a clear container in his city hall office in Lower Manhattan. The "it" Adams was referring to is incorporating plant-based diets citywide—at schools, hospitals, and other public institutions. Overall, public acceptance has been emboldening, he said. So much so that he's making plant-based foods default meals at even more food programs, such as shelters.

"We are going to now look at it in every place that we're feeding people: in our schools, jails, hospitals, child protective custody—all of these places we're saying that at a minimum, we're going to default to plant-based meals and we're going to do initiatives like Meatless Mondays," he said.

Why the fast and broad push? Adams was diagnosed with type 2 diabetes in 2016. He quickly adopted a healthier lifestyle of exercise and vegan dieting. It worked. He lost weight. His vision improved. And he reversed other diabetic symptoms. The vegan cause is obviously very personal to him. He wants to celebrate the benefits of a healthier diet to others, especially inner-city kids who may not have many healthy food options or, for that matter, the understanding to choose healthier foods when presented with them. (When he was Brooklyn Borough president, he forged an effort to eliminate processed foods in schools under a campaign dubbed, "Ban the Boloney.")

What he foresees is making plant-based diets "cool." Otherwise, he said, we are literally feeding chronic disease and destruction of the environment.

"[We] have been almost desensitized to the level of salt and sugar and processed foods that we consume. So, we have to

change our palates—understanding the beauty of tasting and the richness of food. And the initiative for the schools is probably one of the most exciting parts of what we're doing . . . The goal is to have our young people pushing this fight within education. They are open to change. They're really embracing the environment and they've learned how not only carbon emissions from cars are hurting us, but also the emissions that are coming from the overconsumption of meat and dairy and processed foods that we have. So that is our focus, and we are excited about moving this agenda forward," he said eagerly.

How?

"Veganism, vegetarianism, all of those names come with a lot of negative connotations attached to them. And the language is preventing people from embracing the potential. If I were to map out our course for the future: Number one, vegan has to be cool. And that's looking at some high-profile celebrities as speakers. When Beyoncé decided to go plant-based, you know, it just skyrocketed because she's an image builder and many young people look up to her.

"Number two, food must be good for you. It must look good, but darn, it has to taste good. I mean, the Creator made us to enjoy the taste of food so that we can continue as a race for a reason, you know; there's a reason that our palates enjoy food. And so, we want to put a lot of support into making good-tasting, healthy food because that's going to let people see that they can have those cultural norms that they're used to, and they can make a better transition. There are some great chefs out there that I think we need to really support and encourage them to continue to find creative ways to use spices and other cooking methods to make the food really taste good. Because it's one thing to be a plant-based eater or vegan because of moral issues. But if we want people to be on board because of health issues, we've got to start with giving them the palate, the desire that they're looking for.

"Lastly is accessibility and affordability. It's crucial that plant-based foods become accessible and affordable for everyone," he said.

Wouldn't that be, in fact, cool.

Many newspapers reported that environmentalists celebrated the program. But parents? Not so much, it seems. Lots took to social media to express their complaints:

"Most of the kids dumped this in the garbage or just ate the cookies. It smelled like armpits & it was completely unappetizing," wrote one parent. Another posted a photo of some smashed zucchini and corn on a plate with a bag of chips. "The only real meal some of our city's kids can count on is what they get @ school. This wasn't thought through."

How vegan food is cooked and prepared is especially important in making it palatable. Anyone who's had a soggy kelp noodle knows that; we've had our share. But here's the thing: Not every kid likes chicken nuggets. And not every kid hates veggie tacos.

"It's culture wars," Paula Daniels told us. Daniels is the cofounder and chief of What's Next at the Center for Good Food Purchasing, a California nonprofit organization with local partners across the country whose mission is to (re)create a food system that prioritizes the health and well-being of people, animals, and the environment. It focuses on the power of procurement by major institutions. And school meal programs are at the top of the list for reform.

In explaining the importance of school lunch programs, Daniels first pointed to the finding in a report the center produced in association with the Rockefeller Foundation: "School meals provide critical nutrition for 30 million children and their families across America. When children have their basic needs met, they are healthier and they learn better. For them, school meals often provide the healthiest food they have access to each day and a foundation for their well-being and long-term success."

But basic needs aren't being met, and childhood nutrition is lacking. And the planet is suffering from the dietary choices made and the meals served. Why? She said government bureaucracy has a lot to do with it, and a food system that is stiff to change.

"The American geography is based on man's dominion. And I mean that. I chose those words specifically. It's men conquering nature. That's the entirety of America and its expansion—channelizing rivers or dominating animals. We see this, we want it, and we take it. I think that's the underlying issue in the culture wars. They're resisting the idea that you're telling them they can't have something they've always just taken. So I think that's how school lunch programs are caught up in that; it's resistance to change," Daniels said. The entrenchment leaves

NEW GUIDELINES

The current US dietary guidelines expire in 2025, and a new American diet is being planned for 2025–2030 with the advice of nutritionists, researchers, academics, medical professionals, as well as us, the public. We the people can comment directly to the USDA about what we'd like to see (and eat). The USDA.gov website encourages input and has social media forums, a blog, and other collaborative tools to make our diet preferences known.

students burdened with meats, dairy, and high-calorie processed foods, none of which are climate positive.

Daniels said a simple solution would be to match local farms with local schools to provide fresher, healthier, and more climate-friendly meals. She pointed to others, such as Alice Waters, who is also campaigning for

212

this approach and whose efforts were mentioned in chapter seven.

To put a fine point on the benefits, Daniels referenced the numbers and the research from the Rockefeller Foundation: "Momentum has increased toward the benefits of Farm to School, or local sourcing by school districts. Farm to School programs are now in all fifty states and the District of Columbia. Its attendant economic value offers up to $2.16 return for every dollar sourced locally by the school, and up to 2.35 new jobs created in the local region for every job created by a school district in order to focus on local food sourcing (such as a Farm to School coordinator)."

So how can we bring about all these savings? She said the quick answer is to "pay attention." Which, she said, is not so simple at all.

Putting more responsibility on parents isn't fair, but it's needed.

"School board meetings are hard; it takes time off from work," she said. And doing the research to understand how the food system works and who—besides food directors at school districts—can affect change is hard, too. In fact, food directors often have their hands tied, constricted so much by bureaucracy and mandates that they can't make better food choices even if they wanted to.

Still, showing up at school board meetings or initiating letter-writing campaigns can shine a light on issues. Engaging with advocacy organizations and programs is another way. The goal is to get school and public officials to wake up to change and to show there is parental and community support for that change. She explained how her organization does it:

"We ask schools what they are doing about food and how are they using their public dollars? Our motto is public dollars for public goods. We rate them on how they're doing in the criteria of local economy, environmental sustainability, animal welfare, labor, and nutrition. There is a lot of input, and so many

conversations to get the details right. I wouldn't expect the average person to go through that exhausting process. But if the public were to attend parent-teacher association meetings and ask questions and express how much they care about food, that would put wind in our sails."

▲ ▲ ▲ ▲ ▲ ▲ ▲ ▲ ▲

Meal planning for schools isn't just about what kids eat; it's also about what they don't eat. US schools toss an estimated five hundred thousand tons or more of food per year. That comes at a big cost, to the environment and literally: about $10 million per day. Food waste, we now know, is the most common material found at garbage dumps, and when it rots, we also now know, it produces methane, which is even more harmful to the atmosphere than the carbon dioxide pluming from coal plants. Which is why more thought and consideration need to be placed on meal preparation in addition to the types of food purchased for large institutions, as well as what's made at home. Eating all their vegetables is one way for kids to battle food waste. And streamlining huge food buys such as those made by school districts and other big institutions is another.

Meats are usually among the most expensive items on any shopping list, even the government's or schools'. By lessening how much we consume, we might not only save a lot of waste and a lot of money, but we could also reshape the officially recommended American diet. Did you even know

FAST FACT:
We can make our voices known at school meetings and at the voting booth for representatives who support healthier and more planet-friendly meal plans for students.

USDA MyPlate

FOOD GROUP	2 YEAR OLDS	3 YEAR OLDS	4 & 5 YEAR OLDS	WHAT COUNTS AS:
FRUITS	1 c.	1–1½ c.	1–1½ c.	**½ c. of fruit?** ½ c. mashed, sliced, or chopped fruit ½ c. 100% fruit juice ½ medium banana 4–5 strawberries
VEGETABLES	1 c.	1½ c.	1½–2 c.	**½ c. of vegetables?** ½ c. mashed, sliced, or chopped vegetables 1 c. raw leafy greens ½ c. vegetable juice 1 small ear of corn
GRAINS Make half your grains whole	3 oz.	4–5 oz.	4–5 oz.	**1 oz. of grains?** 1 slice of bread 1 c. ready-to-eat cereal flakes ½ c. cooked rice or pasta 1 tortilla (6" across)
PROTEIN FOODS	2 oz.	3–4 oz.	3–5 oz.	**1 oz. of protein foods?** 1 oz. cooked meat, poultry, or seafood 1 egg 1 tbsp. peanut butter ¼ c. cooked beans or peas (kidney, pinto, lentils)
DAIRY Choose low-fat or fat-free	2 c.	2 c.	2½ c.	**½ c. of dairy?** ½ c. milk 4 oz. yogurt ¾ oz. cheese 1 string cheese

Harvard's
ALTERNATE EATING PLAN

Harvard University has taken issue with aspects of the American diet as well and has made it more planet friendly. Harvard issued a report comparing its Healthy Eating Plate to the USDA's MyPlate. Here's what it says we—and namely students—should be eating:

HARVARD'S HEALTHY EATING PLATE

WHOLE GRAINS

"The Healthy Eating Plate encourages consumers to choose whole grains and limit refined grains, since whole grains are much better for health. In the body, refined grains like white bread and white rice act just like sugar. Over time, eating too much of these refined-grain foods can make it harder to control weight and can raise the risk of heart disease and diabetes."

HEALTHY PROTEIN

"The Healthy Eating Plate encourages consumers to choose fish, poultry, beans or nuts, protein sources that contain other healthful nutrients. It encourages them to limit red meat and avoid processed meat since eating even small quantities of these foods on a regular basis raises the risk of heart disease, diabetes, colon cancer, and weight gain."

USDA'S MYPLATE

GRAINS

"Although initially MyPlate did not tell consumers that whole grains are better for health, it has since been revised to suggest that consumers make at least half of their grains whole grains—an important update!"

PROTEIN

"MyPlate's protein section could be filled by a variety of sources, including a hamburger or hot dog. Though the plate has been revised to suggest that adult consumers eat at least 8 ounces of cooked seafood per week, it still offers no indication that red and processed meat are especially harmful to health."

216

HARVARD'S HEALTHY EATING PLATE	USDA'S MYPLATE
VEGETABLES	**VEGETABLES**
"The Healthy Eating Plate encourages an abundant variety of vegetables since Americans are particularly deficient in their vegetable consumption—except for potatoes and French fries. Potatoes are chock full of rapidly digested starch, and they have the same effect on blood sugar as refined grains and sweets, so limited consumption is recommended."	"MyPlate does not distinguish between potatoes and other vegetables."
FRUITS	**FRUITS**
"The Healthy Eating Plate recommends eating a colorful variety of fruits."	"MyPlate also recommends eating fruits."
HEALTHY OILS	**(NOT INCLUDED IN MYPLATE)**
"The Healthy Eating Plate depicts a bottle of healthy oil, and it encourages consumers to use olive, canola, and other plant oils in cooking, on salads, and at the table. These healthy fats reduce harmful cholesterol and are good for the heart, and Americans don't consume enough of them each day. The Healthy Eating Plate also recommends limiting butter and avoiding trans fat."	"MyPlate is silent on fat, which could steer consumers toward the type of low-fat, high-carbohydrate diet that makes it harder to control weight and worsens blood cholesterol profiles."

HARVARD'S HEALTHY EATING PLATE

WATER

"The Healthy Eating Plate encourages consumers to drink water, since it's naturally calorie free, or to try coffee and tea (with little or no sugar), which are also great calorie-free alternatives. It advises consumers to avoid sugary drinks since these are major contributors to the obesity and diabetes epidemics. It recommends limiting milk and dairy to one to two servings per day since high intakes are associated with an increased risk of prostate cancer and possibly ovarian cancer; it recommends limiting juice, even 100% fruit juice, to just a small glass a day, because juice contains as much sugar and as many calories as sugary soda."

STAY ACTIVE

"The figure scampering across the bottom of the Healthy Eating Plate's placemat is a reminder that staying active is half of the secret to weight control. The other half is eating a healthy diet with modest portions that meet your calorie needs."

USDA'S MYPLATE

DAIRY

"MyPlate recommends dairy at every meal, even though there is little if any evidence that high dairy intake protects against osteoporosis, and there is considerable evidence that too-high intakes can be harmful. As for sugary drinks, MyPlate says 100% fruit juice counts as part of the Fruit Group."

(NOT INCLUDED IN MYPLATE)

"There is no activity message on MyPlate."

there was one? Neither did we. But here's what we gleaned from the diet plan laid out by the US Department of Agriculture (USDA):

> Make half your plate fruits and vegetables, and more vegetables than fruits. The other half make grains and protein, and more grain (whole) than protein.

The official USDA recommendation also advises limiting other sources of calories (we're guessing candy and the like) to 240 calories a day.

We learned the USDA-recommended diet is important to students and lots of institutions such as hospitals and prisons because they have to follow the guidelines and purchase their foods accordingly. If more climate-friendly foods were increased as part of the recommended diet, we could do a better job of lessening the planet's fever.

As it stands, the subcategories of food groups such as proteins that we read about in the report are very meat-heavy. We believe the big takeaway of this from a cool food perspective is the recommendation by the USDA that we Americans consume just five ounces of nuts, seeds, or soy products per week as a source of protein versus the twenty-six ounces of either meat, poultry, or eggs. Surely, we can create a better balance

VEGETARIAN OPTIONS

We don't have to go all-veggie to make a difference: we could offset meat or other more carbon-intense food with a cool food choice. Replacing half the animal meat you'd typically serve in a meal with vegetables can reduce that carbon "foodprint" by as much as half.

THE VEGETARIAN GENERATION

A relatively small yet interesting poll of the eating habits of youths aged eight to seventeen revealed more than half of them sometimes or always eat vegetarian meals when eating out. About one in five of them go further and always or sometimes eat vegan. Overall, 5 percent of the American youth population identifies as vegetarian.

there. Nuts and seeds are, of course, leading cool food groups.

We found that more than one hundred countries have national dietary guidelines. Some have made carbon a centerpiece of their recommendations. Denmark, for example, specifically recommends eating more carbon-friendly foods such as fruits, vegetables, and legumes to reduce the carbon emissions associated with food production. It has an ambitious goal of making its entire agricultural industry carbon neutral by 2050.

By our measure, the US could stand to lose some carbon weight and go on a carbon diet of its own. The US dietary guidelines produce the most carbon emissions of any country's recommended diet in the world because of the high amounts of meats and dairy it recommends. India's dietary guidelines, which push people to eat more plant-based proteins, have the smallest footprint.

In our view, fresher and better-tasting options are what we need in the American diet to inform large meal programs such as school lunches. And by allowing students to vote on what they'd like to eat for lunch, some of the approximately 130,000 schools in the US are broadening their proverbial palate. We also found that nonprofit organizations such as the Center for Good Food Purchasing are helping to add better food choices to the mix for kids. Engaging with organizations such as this can help to move the dial in the right direction for students and the planet alike.

Given the trends, planet-friendly foods clearly have an audience. That means more kids might be open to eating cool foods than ever before, and the shift in consumption could better align health and environmental goals.

And what we and our kids eat isn't the only factor at play. Where we buy food for ourselves and our families matters, too. We'll explore those places next.

What You Can Do Today

- **Swap a meat-based lunch for a vegetable-based lunch— even just once a week.**

- **Try replacing half of a meat-centered meal with vegetables and potentially reduce by half the meal's carbon footprint.**

- **Pay more attention to how a meal is prepared. Kids have more taste buds, and certain vegetables—like broccoli—can taste sour in their mouths.**

- **Make your voice known for more planet-friendly lunches at school board meetings, and petition officials who control food programs.**

- **Encourage school programs that allow students to vote on the foods they want to eat.**

- **Get behind nonprofit organizations like the Center for Good Food Purchasing.**

- **Send comments to the USDA, which oversees the American diet and sets guidelines for school lunch programs.**

Recipe courtesy of Vegetarian Society

Avocado and Refried Bean Burrito-Style Wrap

INGREDIENTS

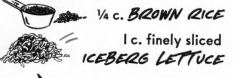 ¼ c. *BROWN RICE*

 1 c. finely sliced *ICEBERG LETTUCE*

 1 large *GREEN ONION*, finely sliced

1 medium *TOMATO*, chopped

 4.38 oz. *CANNED CORN*, drained

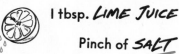 1 *RED CHILI PEPPER* (such as Fresno)

 ¼ c. finely chopped *CILANTRO*

 1 tbsp. *LIME JUICE*

Pinch of *SALT*

 2 large *WHOLE-WHEAT TORTILLAS*

8 oz. canned *REFRIED BEANS*

1 small *AVOCADO*, pitted, skin removed, and sliced

½ c. grated *VEGAN CHEDDAR CHEESE*

METHOD

1 Bring a medium saucepan of water to a boil. Add the brown rice to the pan and cook for about 20 minutes until tender. Drain and then run under cold water to cool.

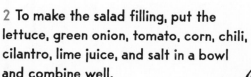

2 To make the salad filling, put the lettuce, green onion, tomato, corn, chili, cilantro, lime juice, and salt in a bowl and combine well.

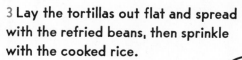

3 Lay the tortillas out flat and spread with the refried beans, then sprinkle with the cooked rice.

4 Place the avocado slices on top of the refried beans and rice and then add the salad.

5 Sprinkle with the cheese and then roll and cut each burrito in half to serve.

237

Recipe courtesy of Vegetarian Society

Tomato Bruschetta with Arugula and Butter Bean Salad

INGREDIENTS

For the Bruschetta:

 3 medium **TOMATOES,** diced

¼ c. torn fresh **BASIL LEAVES**

 ½ small **RED ONION,** finely diced

Pinch of **SALT** and **GROUND BLACK PEPPER**

 I **CLOVE GARLIC,** finely chopped

 4 medium slices **CIABATTA**

For the Salad:

 7 oz. **CANNED BUTTER BEANS,** drained and rinsed

 3 oz. **ARUGULA**

2 tbsp. chopped **ITALIAN PARSLEY**

I tbsp. **LEMON JUICE**

 I small **YELLOW BELL PEPPER,** finely diced

I tbsp. **OLIVE OIL**

METHOD

1 Preheat the broiler to a medium heat.

2 In a bowl, combine the tomatoes, onion, garlic, and basil. Season with salt and pepper. Set aside.

3 In another bowl, add the butter beans, parsley, yellow pepper, arugula, lemon juice, and I tsp. of the olive oil. Season.

4 Toast the ciabatta slices under the broiler until golden brown, about 2 to 4 minutes per side.

5 Once toasted, brush each slice with the remaining olive oil.

6 Spoon the tomato mixture on top of the bread slices and serve with the butter bean salad.

225

SHOPPING

Supermarkets can be climate superheroes. Find the power.

Where you shop for food, we discovered, may be just as important to the climate as the kind of foods you buy. Supermarkets and grocery stores are where the great majority of us purchase our food, and our climate-smart shopping patterns can highlight trends that get food retailers to carry more cool food items. Yet supporting farmers' markets and alternative outlets that stock foods with lower carbon footprints can also forge a more direct line to growers and encourage more planet-friendly crops.

WHERE WE SHOP

Supermarkets and grocery stores are where 92 percent of people in the US get their food. Nearly 5 percent of people get their food from convenience stores. And just over 3 percent get their food from specialty shops, farmers' markets, and the like.

FAST FACTS:
The average family of four on a moderate budget in the United States spends more than $300 per week, topping $1,300 a month on groceries.

When we dove into researching different markets, we were surprised to learn just how many options there are for us to purchase food:

⭐ **Farmers' markets** are where farmers and ranchers usually staff the stalls themselves and explain their products' benefits to individual buyers like you and us. They typically operate one day a week at a specific location in a town or a city neighborhood.

⭐ **Food co-ops** are run by members of a community who typically pay dues and leverage the group's buying power to get better prices on food items, which are usually locally grown. The main idea behind a co-op is to support the local community, so there is an emphasis on purchasing from local growers and food providers.

⭐ **Food hubs** are facilities housed in one location where brokers connect farmers and ranchers to small- and medium-sized buyers, such as specialty grocery stores and local restaurants. The hub manages the sales and accounting that many farmers lack. The general public can visit food hubs most days of the week to shop for locally grown food. Multiple farmers and ranchers drop off their goods at the hub, and the products are source-verified, packaged, and labeled. The hub also oversees the local food supply to maintain adequate quantities and manages this flow for consistency year-round. There are now hundreds of food hubs around the country, and these are a fast-growing segment of the food system throughout the United States as demand for locally sourced food increases.

⭐ **Virtual farmers' markets** are a new way to have direct relationships with local growers and ranchers. The way they work is simple: a vendor lists their items for sale and how much of a product they have to sell at one of the many local farmers'

228

markets' websites. Customers select which items they want, and they have a certain amount of time to purchase. Like a physical farmers' market, there is usually a limited number of days for online buying and selling. Once bought, the items can be shipped directly to a customer's house or the location of the next physical farmers' market in the area when it opens. These virtual markets are important, in our estimation, because growers can reach the masses around the country and reap the benefit of selling more supply. This in turn reduces prices for us all and creates a more efficient system for lesser-known foods, such as cool foods. (Virtual farmers' markets are so important in this regard, we devoted chapter thirteen to them and future foods.)

All that said, while it's good to stock up every week on food from a farmers' market stall to support the growth of cool foods, it's also important to send a strong message to the biggest food buyers in the world. And supermarkets

GROCERY STORE TIP

The food writer Michael Pollan advises shopping in the outside aisles of grocery stores. Fresh foods, and therefore more organic and climate-friendly foods, are likely stocked there. Processed and packaged foods are typically stocked closer to the center of a supermarket, Pollan notes.

and convenience stores are, as noted, key food drivers.

We asked Richard Waite, a senior research associate at the World Resources Institute and the author of the WRI report *Creating a Sustainable Food Future*, to tell us more about the retailer perspective on this and what retailers can do to improve their cool food attitude. From inside WRI's offices in Washington, DC, less than two miles from the Department of Agriculture, he explained that basic

preferences are the levers to changing the food system as we know it.

"Taste, pricing, and convenience probably override everything," Waite said. "So, within a shopping environment, whether you're talking about a supermarket or a restaurant, any effort to encourage more climate-friendly food should probably take that into account.

"When you think about a supermarket environment, maybe putting the climate-friendly foods in prominent locations is one thing. When those plant-based meat alternatives first came out, people were putting them in the alternative food section, or the organic section of the healthy food section. But now a lot of times you see it right there next to the meat counter. And that's where the traffic is. More of that, I think, would actually be a really powerful thing. Then there's the opposite of it, too, right? If there are things that are higher [carbon] emitting, maybe you want to encourage

a bit less selection. It's putting the more sustainable stuff front and center."

Waite said carbon labeling can help muster attention to more climate-friendly foods, too, but only to a point.

"We do know that just labeling things isn't going to be a silver bullet. We've had nutrition facts everywhere for decades, and still, we haven't solved all of our nutritional issues. But it's something that could help," he said. (We'll dive more into carbon labeling in chapter twelve.) "I think we need to be thinking about how we make the climate-friendly products as tasty, as affordable, as convenient, as high-quality, and as desirable as the things that they're replacing."

The most sustainable food choice lies with the actual food itself and how it's grown or raised.

"Most of the food-related emissions happen before the food ever leaves the farm versus how far it traveled or how it's packaged. And so, eating local and meeting your farmer are good for other

THE EVOLUTION OF THE GROCERY STORE

The first known farmers' market in the United States was opened in Boston. It reportedly opened in 1634 and was quickly followed by others in the early colonies.

From there, farmers' markets began to move west for several centuries along with the expansion of the States. The federal government sponsored the first farmers co-op in the early 1900s, and the first commercial grocery was opened soon after: in 1916, the Piggly Wiggly market in Memphis, Tennessee, allowed customers to choose items from store shelves. Until then, stores would prepare items for customers on request. It should also be noted that most grocers at the time only sold dry goods such as flour and sugar and canned items. It wasn't until the King Kullen market opened in 1936 in Queens that meats, produce, dry goods, and baked items were sold in one store. The shopping cart was invented around the same time, and the many choices and the power for customers to choose items themselves brought along advertising and specials and promotions, the hallmarks of the grocery store and supermarket as we know them today. If only we could extend promotions to cooler foods.

WHAT IS A TERMINAL MARKET?

A terminal market is also called a "central market" and refers to a place for food products or technically any commodity that is received from scattered outlying locations and sold to the public. While we the public can buy food at these complexes, many are designed for volume sales to retailers.

reasons. They're not a major climate strategy," he said. The biggest climate positives are the shift from animal proteins, especially beef and lamb, toward plant-based foods.

And the message itself needs to be positive.

"One catchphrase that I like and that we use sometimes in our cool food program is 'delicious climate action.' It doesn't have to be just about doing less of what we like or overhauling our lifestyles, but it can be kind of one meal at a time. 'Hey, I did something good.' Or, 'I did something less bad than I could've done.' If you talk about celebrating what you're shifting towards and the benefits of plants and how, you know, beautiful and delicious and all of that that they are, then shifting towards plants can be perceived as more palatable than eating less meat," Waite said.

Yet the changes and the messaging must be forged by myriad influencers—including each of us.

"It's hard to do. But when you're getting to some of these large food companies, whether they're supermarkets or food service companies or manufacturers, they shape what we

FAST FACT:
Philadelphia's Reading Terminal Market has been part of the city's fabric since 1893 and prides itself on serving hometown fare.

"Hunts Point is a public market, but few people take advantage of it, I'm told. And I understand why. It's intimidating to enter through the tall interstate-highway-like toll gates in the Bronx. Eighteen-wheeler trucks come and go. The neighborhood is industrial, not very welcoming like a Sunday farmers' market at your local, suburban high school might be. Scrap metal, body shops, and various light-machinery operators surround the massive complex. Run-down buildings. Graffiti. You get the picture.

"Around thirty food companies truck, ship, and freight-train their goods to this terminal market. (Terminal markets got their name, I was informed by one produce vendor, because they were the last stop on the train—where it terminated.) There aren't individual vendor stalls per se. Each has a booth at the dock, where the goods are unloaded. That's where buyers come at night.

"'You gotta come at eleven [p.m.] or four in the morning, that's when the real action is,' Mike, a seller for one of the major food companies, tells me in exactly the type of thick Bronx accent you'd expect. Scrums of buyers from markets, large and small, bodegas, grocery stores, and supermarkets cut and taste—to find out how a particular fruit or vegetable 'eats'— and bid on various fruits and vegetables that they'll buy by the box. But anyone can come in and get the same wholesale prices. It's something that more people should take advantage of—at any terminal market. Prices are cheaper than farmers' markets, and you're still getting farm-direct food."

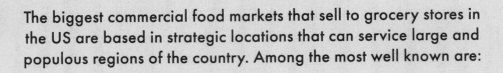

Where Grocery Stores Shop

The biggest commercial food markets that sell to grocery stores in the US are based in strategic locations that can service large and populous regions of the country. Among the most well known are:

- Philadelphia's Reading Terminal Market

- Los Angeles's Terminal Market at Seventh Street

- Chicago's South Water Market

- New York's Hunts Point Produce Market

- St. Louis Produce Market

- Oakland (California) Produce Market

- Plant City (Florida) State Farmers' Market

- Maryland Wholesale Produce Market

eat in a lot of ways. And then you don't wanna rule out government. One of the interesting things that we are seeing in our cool food program is at the city level, where they are willing to do interesting things like shifting their public procurement," Waite said.

Food systems are complicated. If you show up in a big marketplace and you start saying that you want more organic, he explained that demand has to be there, volume has to be there, and quality has to be there. Otherwise, taste, price, and convenience won't be there—and the system falls apart.

He said, "There has to be some sort of shared vision. Otherwise, farmers will say, 'I'm only going to grow what people will buy from me.' And [corporate] buyers will say, 'I'm only going to sell what people will buy from me.' And customers will say, 'I'm only going to buy what's available.'"

We learned that there is a bit of a leapfrog trick that can help get the climate message to grocery-store and supermarket buyers: We can visit wholesale markets that also service commercial stores, and buy foods directly. This not only coaxes sellers to carry more climate-smart foods; it also can raise awareness of the cool food movement and bring attention to our demand for said foods to the big food buyers.

Many supermarkets and large store chains get their food directly from growers or ranchers. They keep their own distribution centers and dispatch food accordingly. But most retail grocery stores aren't big enough to do that on their own, we learned, so they turn to wholesale markets where vendors can give them better prices based on the cumulative volume of the many stores they sell to. Most of us only get a taste of what giant commercial markets are like when we visit our local farmers' market. Wholesale commercial food markets are massive. Some are even bigger than entire cities. They're worth visiting.

The most amount of food gets

235

distributed through New York's Hunts Point market in the Bronx. Others may reign in terms of size, revenue, or sales, but Hunts Point has the world's highest volume of food that is delivered and shipped. The market, which moved from Washington Street in Manhattan in 1967, clocks sales of $2 billion per year and sits on sixty acres along the Harlem River. It hums every day, twenty-four seven.

Hunts Point is a cooperative, meaning each vendor is an owner of the market—so meat distributors get just as much of a say in how the market is run as vegetable distributors. But one voice is clearly missing among the crowd: organic foods. Even though there are miles of produce to be had, we found that few vendors have organic products, never mind cool foods.

This is where and how we can voice our support for organics by the types of food purchases we make. Food markets like Hunts Point are where pretty much everything that we eat gets decided.

Which kinds of cereals make it onto the store shelves and eventually into our bowls at the breakfast table at home; what vegetables end up on display and in our shopping baskets; the different types of milk in the refrigerator section; and much, much more, spanning every food aisle. Whether we know it or not, our preferences are limited and determined at food stalls that service commercial food operators. By showing up at wholesale markets and ginning up demand for cool foods, we can help shift our food fate.

We had a chance to talk to quite a few people at Hunts Point, starting with Phillip Grant, the CEO of Hunts Point Produce Market, the world's largest distribution center for fruits and vegetables.

"Where we're located in the supply chain is very unique," he said. "We're an ecosystem. If one thing falls apart, the whole system falls apart."

Conversely, when positive change occurs, it spreads through the whole

produce community, which includes growers, truckers, distribution centers, and grocery stores. Changes in the food system ripple and shift habits. And sustainability is forging big change, he said. It extends from the types of foods grown and how they're grown, to more efficient transportation and refrigeration, to the way Hunts Point itself operates, eyeing any and every way to reduce its energy use and step up considerations for food waste.

All that said, Grant relayed that it's no easy feat to tilt the food system toward a more climate-friendly diet. There are so many moving parts, so many pieces to the puzzle. Still, he realizes that the food supply has to become much more sustainable. Food waste, water issues, even organics and more eco-friendly growing practices will all take a back seat to consumer demand. It starts and stops there, he said, full circle.

"Customers decide what sells," said Gabriela D'Arrigo, vice president of marketing and communications for D'Arrigo, one of Hunts Point's largest produce vendors, with operations around the country and thousands of acres of farmland. At the moment, organics are continuing to trend, and in the future, she sees tropical fruits taking center stage. "When I started in the industry ten years ago, growers dictated what was going to be sold. 'This is what we grow,' they said. 'This is what's going to be sold. This is what you're going to take.' About three years into my career in this industry, that changed significantly. All of a sudden, consumers were starting to say no. The health trends were starting. Veganism was coming into play. A lot of people were becoming vegetarians. They were like, 'No, I wanna have more variety. I wanna have more of this kind of healthy item.' And then that led to the organics. So that's kind of when it started to really pick up. At the same time, chefs became the new rock stars. Every social media platform gave them a voice. Social media, by the way, is a huge catalyst for us and dictates a lot of what

ORGANIC DEMAND

Organics—despite the rise of Whole Foods and similar markets—make up just 6 percent of total US food sales. Yet 45 percent of Americans believe organic food is healthier, and 67 percent are concerned about the impact of food production on climate change.

growers grow. So now we're constantly in communication with all of the retailers across the country and internationally saying, 'This is what consumers are asking for,'" D'Arrigo said.

Vendors like D'Arrigo are able to predict coming trends. For instance, the rise in tropical fruits that she mentioned is correlated to the rise in the number of immigrants coming into the US from tropical areas. "That's going to be a trend five, ten years down the road," she said. Imported produce, too, will rise: "The biggest concern that we

have is there's not any more land here in the United States. That's a big reason why a lot of stuff is being imported. A lot of the land that is here has been completely depleted of nutrients, and it's not properly utilized. So, there's not a lot of proper crop rotation happening to put nutrients back into the soil. For example, cauliflower and broccoli take a lot of nutrients out of the soil. You need to crop rotate with berries, something light, something that's a little bit more nutritious to put nutrients back into the soil. But too often that doesn't happen," D'Arrigo said.

No matter where or how food is grown, the ultimate arbiter of supply is taste, said Stefanie Katzman, executive vice president at Katzman Produce, another big Hunts Point food distributor. "So," she said, "speak up when something tastes good. I always tell people, ask your produce manager in the store that you go in and shop in because the produce manager— especially in some of the smaller stores, like not your big corporate chains—they're usually the ones doing the ordering. And if they know someone wants something, they'll ask us. And guess what? We'll go out and find it or grow it. That's how things change."

While shopping at a wholesale market can have a larger impact, we know that it's far easier and more convenient to hit the supermarket. And sending a soft message by shopping or giving props to growers and local farmers may not be enough to get more cool foods into the US food system. This is where feedback can come into play.

We're all used to—and likely annoyed by—the "we'd love to hear from you" or "your opinion matters" surveys that end up in our email inbox after we purchase something or use a service. But these surveys are where we can express our desire for more sustainable choices and cool foods. Social media presents other opportunities. We found that most grocery stores have their own social media handle that we can message directly. We can also begin a petition for more cool foods by using a hashtag.

And here's a little fact we found that could get more company sales turned onto cool foods: Most of us, according to the data, are willing to pay more for climate-friendly food. This should give retailers room to provide us with more cool food even if it's more expensive.

We're not suggesting that cool foods should cost that much more than traditional food fare. But suppliers should know that, along with our bigger appetites for climate-friendly food, we might have bigger budgets for it.

How much we're willing to spend on food and our desire for quality food here in the United States probably seem

> **FAST FACT:**
> We need to shop more at farmers' markets. There are approximately 8,000 farmers' markets in the United States versus more than 63,000 grocery stores and supermarkets.

WHAT WOULD YOU PAY?

Research surveys show that people are willing to pay higher prices for milk, bread, and meat—as much as 50 percent over usual prices. Coffee is the next item people are willing to pay more for, just under half as much more. Then it's bottled water (46.7 percent) and vegetables (47.2 percent).

outsized. But we learned the average American spends the least amount on food as a percentage of their income than anyone else in the world. We Americans spend an average of 6.4 percent of our household income on food, whereas someone in Nigeria, for example, spends more than 40 percent of what they earn on food, according to the research. In our next chapter, we'll see how food systems favor more developed countries and how cool food can be incorporated into diets around the world.

What You Can Do Today

- Try shopping at farmers' markets and co-ops.
- Check out online food hubs that combine foods from different locations into one order.
- Visit a terminal market.
- Purchase and request more organic foods.
- Use social media, surveys, and other means of informing food retailers of your desire for more climate-friendly foods.
- Take the food writer Michael Pollan's advice and stick to the outside aisles of supermarkets and grocery stores. That's where you'll likely find fresh, organic foods that are more climate friendly.

Recipe courtesy of Vegetarian Society

Pulled Jackfruit Flatbread Wraps

INGREDIENTS

For the Pulled Jackfruit:

2 tbsp. *DARK BROWN SUGAR*

1 tsp. *SALT*

½ tbsp. *SMOKED PAPRIKA*

1 tsp. *CAYENNE PEPPER*

1 *CHIPOTLE PEPPER IN ADOBO*, minced into a paste

3 (14 oz. each) cans *JACKFRUIT*, drained

1½ c. *VEGETABLE BROTH*

For the Flatbreads:

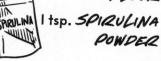

2 c. *WHOLE-WHEAT FLOUR*

½ c. all-purpose *FLOUR*

1 tsp. *SPIRULINA POWDER*

¼ tsp. *SALT*

⅓ c. plus 1 tbsp. *WARM WATER*

2 tbsp. *CANOLA OIL*

For the Coleslaw:

1 small *CARROT*, peeled and cut into matchsticks

¼ small *RED CABBAGE*, shredded

¼ small *GREEN CABBAGE*, shredded

¼ *RED APPLE*, cored and cut into matchsticks

1 tsp. unfiltered *APPLE CIDER VINEGAR*

½ tsp. *SALT*

1 tbsp. *VEGAN GREEK-STYLE YOGURT*

2 tbsp. *VEGAN MAYONNAISE*

1 tsp. *WHOLE-GRAIN MUSTARD*

To Fill the Wraps:

1 (16-oz.) can small *WHITE BEANS*, such as navy or cannellini, rinsed and drained

Handful of *WATERCRESS* or *ARUGULA*

Toasted *SUNFLOWER SEEDS*

241

METHOD

Decide the cooking method:

1 Both the jackfruit and the flatbreads can be cooked in a regular oven, on the stovetop, or, for a smokier flavor, on the barbecue or in a pizza oven. The temperature should always be around 300°F, so make sure to keep an eye on that if using the last two options.

To make the pulled jackfruit:

2 In a large bowl, add brown sugar, salt, smoked paprika, cayenne pepper, and minced chipotle, and combine well. Add the drained jackfruit and toss all the ingredients together. Cover the bowl in plastic wrap and place in the fridge.

3 Place the marinated jackfruit in a casserole dish. Add the vegetable broth, stir, and cover with a lid or tightly cover with aluminum foil. Place it in the oven or on the grill for 40 minutes. If using a grill or pizza oven, make sure during the cooking that the temperature stays around 300°F. If during the cooking it looks too dry, add a small amount of stock.

To make the flatbreads:

4 In a large mixing bowl, add the two types of flour, spirulina, and salt. In a measuring cup, combine the warm water and *canola oil. Slowly add the wet ingredients into the dry ingredients, while combining with your hand. A food processor can also be used for this.

*for best results add 1–2 tbsp. extra canola oil

5 Knead the dough for 4–5 minutes, until smooth. Wrap the dough in plastic wrap and set aside.

OR

243

To make the coleslaw:

6 Combine all the vegetables and fruits in a mixing bowl, add the vinegar and salt, and let sit for 5 minutes. Add the yogurt, mayonnaise, and mustard, and mix well. Cover with plastic wrap and set aside in the fridge.

7 Remove the jackfruit from the oven, which will be now fully cooked. Shred the jackfruit into strips using two forks.

To make the wraps:

8 Unwrap the dough and cut it into 4 pieces. Start flattening a quarter on a floured surface, using a rolling pin to stretch it until it is 0.03 inch thick and 10 inches in diameter. Repeat the process with the other 3 dough pieces.

9 If using the hot oven, add the flatbreads, one by one, and flip them over after around 4 minutes. Cook for a further 4 minutes. If using the stovetop, place the flatbreads in a dry frying pan over high heat and cook on both sides for 4 minutes.

To assemble the wraps:

10 On a plate, place your flatbread, and add the beans, jackfruit, coleslaw, some watercress or arugula, and a sprinkle of toasted sunflower seeds. Roll up the wraps tightly to finish.

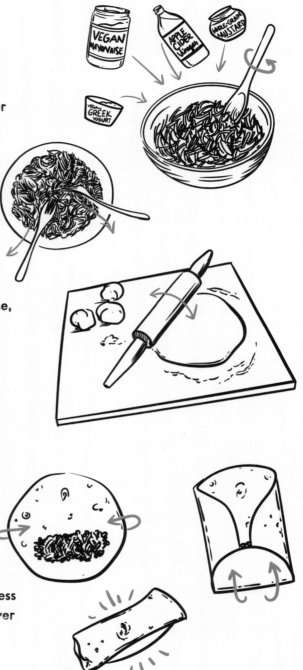

Recipe courtesy of Vegetarian Society

Pasta with Ragū and Winter Slaw

INGREDIENTS

For the Ragù:

1 tbsp. **CANOLA OIL**

1 **CELERY STALK**, finely chopped

1 small **CARROT**, peeled and finely chopped

1 small **ONION**, peeled and finely chopped

1 **GARLIC** clove, peeled and finely chopped

 2 **BAY LEAVES**

 1 tsp. dried **SAGE**

 1 tsp. dried **THYME**

 1 tsp. dried **BASIL**

 ¾ c. cooked **BROWN LENTILS**, from a can or packet

 1 tbsp. **TOMATO PASTE**

 7 oz. **CRIMINI MUSHROOMS**, roughly chopped

 ¾ c. **WALNUTS**, chopped

 ¾ c. low-sodium **VEGETABLE BROTH**

 1 tbsp. aged **BALSAMIC VINEGAR**

 1 (14-oz.) can petite diced or **STRAINED TOMATOES**

 ¼ c. chopped **ITALIAN PARSLEY**

 **SALT** and **PEPPER**, to taste

For the Pappardelle:

14 oz. dried **PAPPARDELLE**

245

For the Winter Slaw:

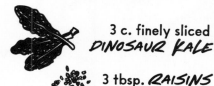

3 c. finely sliced *DINOSAUR KALE*

3 tbsp. *RAISINS*

2 small *CARROTS,* peeled and shaved

¼ small *RED CABBAGE,* shaved

1 tbsp. *CANOLA OIL*

1 tsp. *ENGLISH MUSTARD*
(Colman's mustard can be purchased online or wherever you can buy imported groceries)

1 *LEMON,* zest and juice

¼ tsp. *SALT*
½ tsp. *PEPPER*

To Serve:

¼ c. chopped *ITALIAN PARSLEY*

1 c. grated vegetarian *ITALIAN-STYLE HARD CHEESE*

247

METHOD
To make the ragù:

1 In a large frying pan, add the canola oil and fry the celery, carrot, and onion over medium heat for 5 minutes, until translucent.

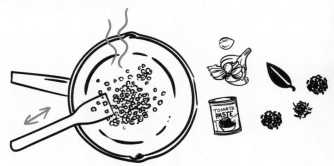

2 Add the garlic, bay leaves, and all the dried herbs. Continue cooking for 3 minutes. Add the tomato paste and cook for 3 minutes.

3 Add the chopped mushrooms and cook for 15 minutes. Add the walnuts and lentils, then cook for 5 minutes.

4 Add the vegetable broth, balsamic vinegar, and diced or strained tomatoes and cook for 15–20 minutes, until the sauce has thickened. Add the Italian parsley. Season to taste.

To make the pappardelle:

5 In a saucepan, bring 3⅓ cups water to a boil. Add the pappardelle and simmer for 10 minutes or until the pasta is cooked.

To make the winter slaw:

6 Place the dinosaur kale and raisins into a colander inside a large bowl. Boil a teakettle and pour hot water over them to soften. When soft, lift the colander out to drain.

7 In a bowl, mix together the dinosaur kale, raisins, carrot, and cabbage.

To make the winter slaw dressing:

8 In a separate bowl, combine all the remaining winter slaw ingredients and mix together thoroughly. Add the dressing to the vegetables and raisins.

To serve:

9 Toss the pasta into the ragù and put it on a large serving platter. Top the ragù with the extra parsley and grated Italian-style hard cheese. Serve with the winter slaw on the side.

INTERNATIONAL MARKETS

There's a butterfly effect in your soup. Eat it up.

Why do we care what or how anyone anywhere else around the world grows or consumes food? We should care because food, despite the big push for locally grown products, is a global commodity. That means no matter where something is grown or eaten in the world, it affects us at home. *C'mon, how is that possible?* you're likely thinking, skeptically. We questioned this butterfly effect, too. But it turns out that it's true. Consider that most of our fruits and a quickly rising amount of our vegetables—about a third, as noted elsewhere in these pages—are imported, and the link to foreign food markets becomes easier to understand. If the foods from these countries are better or worse for our health and the planet, it's in our best interest to know. Yet figuring out which food comes from where, and whether that food is climate friendly, isn't so clear. However, we learned that things are changing, and we may soon be able to make food shopping decisions based on where and

FAST FACT: India has more plants (45,000 different species) than any other country in the world. Yet Brazil is the world's most biodiverse, with a huge array of plants and animals.

251

International Supply

In the US, our largest trading partners are Mexico and Canada, and we have preferred trading arrangements with them to make goods less costly. In terms of food, we found that . . .

From Mexico, we import avocados along with other fruits and vegetables.

From Canada, we import processed foods, certain grains, and red meat.

From Europe, we get lots of nuts and melons.

From Asia, we get lots of our processed fruits and vegetables, as well as snack foods.

From South America, we get lots of our tree nuts, beans, and coffee.

Because we import so much fruit from Mexico, from that perspective they are our most climate-friendly trading partner.

252

how foods are grown just as readily as we can on prices.

The price of food, of course, is linked to global supply and demand. The data shows that after oil and gas, food is the most traded commodity in the world. And corn tops the list of food commodities, followed by soybeans, raw sugar, and winter wheat. When overseas growers don't have enough, say, wheat to send to the market, and local buyers corner as much of the market as they can, a loaf of bread at your local grocery store becomes a lot more valuable—and pricey. (Most bread is made from wheat flour.) We saw the stark reality of this when Russia invaded Ukraine—a major exporter of wheat—and the price of wheat went up more than 50 percent.

There is the opposite of this pricing situation, too. If overseas growers can increase—and diversify—their supply of, for instance, cool foods, prices may be more welcoming here in the United States, and that may incentivize buyers to stock up on things like nuts, berries, and syrups. Which is where all our shopping habits come into play.

This happened with seafood. We learned that more seafood is selling because of trade agreements between countries that allow more fish to be imported or exported without, or with lower, tariffs and taxes, among other factors. So, we're wondering, why couldn't we do the same "free trade" for cool foods? If we could incentivize

THE WORLD TRADE ORGANIZATION

The World Trade Organization, which oversees the rules for the trading of food and other goods between countries, may only have been formed in 1995, but it can trace its history back some seventy years to when the General Agreement on Tariffs and Trade (GATT) was signed. The GATT was created after the world wars to lower trade barriers and mitigate protectionism—in which nations horde goods and excessively tax imports to "protect" domestic producers like farmers. Signed in the aftermath of World War II and the Bretton Woods Agreement that established a new monetary world order, the GATT brought about more trade over decades and enlisted more and more countries to participate. After a meeting in 1993 in Uruguay, in which 125 countries participated, the WTO was created to subsume the GATT and to figure out ways to increase global trade more fairly.

Today, the World Trade Organization is composed of most of the world's countries. It helps to bring governments together to decide on trading rules that benefit everyone. Its mission is to lower barriers to trade and to help less-developed countries participate in world markets. It also aims to create fairer competition, taking into account the protection of the environment. It oversees all kinds of products, food top among them.

By importing and exporting food, we wage major influence around the globe. How much we grow and consume of one kind of food can make a world market. Indeed, a world market oriented around cool food could help save the planet. And it's partly up to the WTO to help make that happen.

governments to allow freer and more supply of climate-friendly foods to trade in the world market, a lot of the work to reduce climate change could be taken care of for us. The supply would create growth opportunities for farmers while at the same time drawing and storing more carbon from the atmosphere.

It's easy to feel powerless in the global trade policy system. As individuals, we can't make policy. But we can express our desire for better policies via the politicians for whom we vote, and we can advocate for better policies such as lowering taxes on carbon-friendly foods and increasing them on carbon-intense foods. That strategy would allow cool foods to compete better on the world stage.

The World Trade Organization negotiates balances like this as part of its mission. And a report we read examined different scenarios for how the organization could help the planet through more favorable trade agreements. Like us, it got stuck on the

Fair-Trade Certified

Fair-trade certified products that are labeled as such are those that claim to be more ethically made or grown, meaning that fairer wages are paid to workers and environmental and social conditions are taken into account in the production process. For food, it can also mean that smaller farms are given the opportunity to participate in global trade—affording them more opportunities to prosper.

politics of it all. However, it did uncover a powerful possibility that all of us could get behind: carbon labeling. By knowing how much carbon emissions it takes to make a product, our choice of climate-friendly foods at the checkout counter would be made far easier and could send a strong message around the world about our preferences. Such labeling, according to the WTO, could be akin to the

"organic" and "fair trade" labels, which help us make decisions based on other factors and which have become popular.

We learned that the organic and fair-trade food markets are booming because more people are choosing items that better reflect their personal values—and that includes caring for the planet. We believe a carbon label could also be an easy thing to spot and help us care for the climate. So how can we get more labels onto items? Food companies have to hear from us.

Some have already begun using them. Unilever, for instance, has committed to putting a carbon footprint label on all its products—a massive amount of detail considering that it produces tens of thousands of items sold in 190 countries around the world. With brands such as Ben & Jerry's ice cream, Hellmann's mayonnaise, Knorr, and dozens more, its impact could be industry changing, across numerous industries. And Unilever is thinking about how to make their food cooler in other ways as well, like making more vegan products available.

"I certainly feel a responsibility as a company, as a big foods company, to see how we can make vegan or vegetarian alternatives easy and fun for consumers," Hanneke Faber, the president of Nutrition at Unilever, told us. Faber is responsible for sourcing food from farm to shelf and ensuring its health, nutrition, and sustainability.

"We should help that decision; it shouldn't be hard," Faber said. "A great example is Ben & Jerry's [vegan ice cream]. It's dairy-free and totally delicious. You don't have to make any changes in your habits. You can still sit on the couch and pig out on a pint. It is totally delicious, and it is a product that doesn't depend on cows. You can still have your favorite taste, but it doesn't depend on animals.

"We've also done some acquisitions. We bought a little brand here in Europe. [Faber is based in Amsterdam.] It's called the Vegetarian Butcher. And it's doing really well in vegetarian burgers and chicken pieces. It's the [veggie] Whopper for Burger King. It's the [veggie] chicken nuggets for Burger King. That's all by the Vegetarian Butcher. So again, then people don't have to change their habits. They can still go to Burger King and really enjoy a great vegan burger. If everyone were to do a bit of that, it will make a big difference to the planet."

To be sure, sales of vegetarian and vegan products in Europe far exceed those in the United States, by as much as 400 percent in some cases. Faber attributed this to US consumer demand lagging other regions of the world. Throughout Asia, vegetarian food is already a big component of meals. Europe is changing fast. In the US, growth is steady yet incremental. She said, "It just takes time for people to change their habits. And it's one plate at a time. So, yes, there are a lot of US consumers who want it, but we have the responsibility to make it easier and more accessible. It's going to be a little tighter financially for many

FAST FACT:
Certain companies are adding QR codes on packaging. Scan the code with a smartphone to see how much carbon it took to make the item throughout its life cycle.

people in the months ahead, and we're also going to make sure all of our food is affordable."

The economic matrix to source fresh yet less expensive products is more difficult outside of the USA because certain countries don't have a diverse bounty within their own borders. They are at the mercy of others, and that takes a lot of cost management.

Faber said the US is in a unique position compared to other countries when it comes to food. She said in many ways "it's a pretty self-sufficient country." Indeed, the vast majority of the ingredients Unilever sources for its food products come from US farmers. Which could help move things more

The COOL Label

As we mentioned in chapter seven, grocery stores and supermarkets are required by law to show where many foods are grown or raised. The Country of Origin Labeling (COOL) law requires stores to "notify" consumers about the country of origin for "muscle cuts and ground lamb, chicken, goat, wild and farm-raised fish and shellfish, perishable agricultural commodities (vegetables), peanuts, pecans, ginseng, and macadamia nuts."

quickly toward a vegetarian-centric US diet. The supply is already here. The big question becomes enticing demand and diversifying food selections. To bring that about, Unilever's brand Knorr began the Future 50 Foods initiative. (Check out the Future 50 Foods list at the back of the book.)

"It was really inspired by the fact that all of us on the planet really only eat twelve plants and five animals. And obviously there's a lot more diversity of what one can eat. It's food for one's own health, and it's also very good for the earth because soils benefit from growing different things. So, we work with WWF [World Wide Fund for Nature] and with WRI [World Resources Institute] to provide a guide to foods that we should eat more of because they're high in nutrients, take less resources, and use less water to grow. We've been using that list with chefs and with Knorr itself. It really acts as a guide to create new products and swaps. One of our biggest products on Knorr is a spaghetti Bolognese mix. We now do that with lentils rather than with minced meat. That's a simple swap . . . But some are a little harder to get people to adopt—things like teff and finger millet. We have a big program now actually in Africa on finger millet because that's a great crop for soil and for people," Faber said.

The challenge is getting people all over the world to eat food to which they are unaccustomed. But Faber said she and Unilever are up to the job: "We're going to keep hammering away at the Future 50 to see if we can diversify diets."

It shouldn't be hard, but it is.

Still, smaller brands are getting into the act as well. They're finding that adding carbon labels drives sales. According to an article we read in *Fast Company* magazine, Just Salad, a restaurant chain, saw its sales jump when it added carbon counts to its menu, and Oatly (the world's largest oat milk company) even uses a carbon footprint label as a brand differentiator.

These are voluntary efforts by just a few climate-conscious companies. That makes it difficult to look at one product versus another—as with calorie counts that are on all products—and compare

which is better or worse. For the time being, the onus is on us as shoppers to do the homework and pick the best products for the planet.

We toured numerous grocery stores and found that while *where* something is grown is sometimes shown, *how* food is grown is rarely detailed. This information isn't just useful for us consumers; it's useful for companies as well.

"Those [companies] that do examine their products' life cycle often realize that there are [ingredient] swaps they can make or make transport improvements that usually both reduce carbon and save costs," said Matthew Isaacs, cofounder and business director of My Emissions, a firm that enables companies and individuals to calculate the carbon emissions of their foods as well as entire recipes. "Those savings can accrue to the climate in the form of lower carbon emissions and to us consumers (theoretically) in the form of lower prices."

Over a (what else?) vegetable salad lunch at a sidewalk café in London's

> **FAST FACT:**
> My Emissions offers a carbon calculator for food on its website, MyEmissions.green. Try it.

Carbon Footprint Labels

Carbon footprint labels detail CO_2 as CO_2e, which means carbon dioxide equivalent. CO_2e is used to show the number of metric tons of greenhouse gas emissions with the same global warming potential. It is meant to be used as a uniform measuring stick for multiple greenhouse gases. Labels can include this total to detail manufacturing, production, distribution, as well as end-of-life amounts. Some labels take the subcategories and detail them even further (e.g. packaging) and provide recycling and other instructions.

Notting Hill, he said, "One small swap can make a massive difference. One meal going from beef to not even vegetarian or vegan, just beef to chicken or other lower-carbon meals can make a real big impact on the environment.

And if everyone started using that mentality, we could really make a difference. All of that feedback could be fed back through the system and could ensure that we ended up with a more sustainable food system over time."

In that scenario, what would happen, he explained, is food companies would quickly get the message that they could create enormous efficiencies across their entire supply chain—something that isn't occurring as standard operating procedure today. Those who have made efforts to create supply chain transparency often find big opportunities for savings, in terms of both carbon emissions as well as costs.

My Emissions maps the full journey of food products from the ground to the shelf. It starts with the literal earth and the inert carbon storage potential of a raw food item, whether plant or animal. Depending on how much data is available, this becomes a positive or negative potential: cattle, for instance, being immediately (and significantly) negative, while a plant would assume (generally) a more climate-positive attribute. Then each phase of processing and production, as well as storage and transportation, is calculated to arrive at a detailed rating.

More and more food companies are choosing to calculate their carbon food counts because of consumer demand for more climate information and the prospect that carbon labeling will become mandated much like nutrition labels, Isaacs said. Carbon labels, he predicted, will likely become mandatory in the European Union and the United Kingdom and then make their way across the Atlantic to the US as policy.

The most challenging aspect of the carbon analysis process, Isaacs said, is gathering good data on specific foods' carbon storage potential. The reason is that different locations where food is grown may have different soil types, farming processes, or weather conditions that can affect exactly how much carbon a plant stores.

"I would say that of all the calculations, that's one where there is more uncertainty," he said. "Things like measuring land use, which changes the actual sequestration of carbon, is more uncertain. It's slightly harder to measure, but we do still try to do it because we feel that's the right thing to do."

With thousands of food types in the My Emissions database, which group has the lowest carbon footprint?

"Generally, fruits and vegetables or grains when they are in season have the lowest carbon footprint," Isaacs said. But there is a caveat. "When you're looking at scale, those foods are really important. But there's nutrition, too, and making sure that you're not just trying to get the lowest carbon food, but food that is actually fresh and nutritious."

FAST FACT:
Organic and fair-trade labels are informative but not always good assessments of whether something is planet friendly.

What's surprising to most people and companies, Isaacs said, is that it's the food itself that has the biggest climate impact.

"Usually, the biggest surprise is how big an impact farming and processing has for a product when compared to its transportation or its packaging. Farming and processing can often be more than fifty percent and more likely sixty, seventy, eighty percent of a food's carbon footprint. We sometimes see transport and packaging is as little as five percent of a food's carbon footprint. But in the media, and generally, when you hear about carbon emissions, a lot of it is about plastics or it's about transportation. Well, actually, both of those areas have far, far lower impacts on the planet than agriculture and farming and the production of our foods. It's the food choices that we make. It's the foods we're eating. It's the ingredients we're using. These generally have a much larger impact on the environment

than where it's coming from or how it's packed. A lot of our work is trying to educate our customers that actually, yes, you can change your packaging, but if you've got a product that's focused on beef, and even if you've got the best beef, it is likely going to have a very large carbon price," he said.

To be sure, some companies celebrate how their products are grown or made. Patagonia, for example, recently began selling food under its "Provisions" label and provides details about the small farms from where it sources foods. In fact, Patagonia has been known to use QR codes to show videos of how a product made it from origin to shelf; it's a neat thing to check out. Moreover, Patagonia is championing an entirely new food certification label: Regenerative Organic Certified. That label, according

to the company, means the food was grown on a farm that practices organic and regenerative agriculture. Regenerative agriculture is a way of farming that focuses on maintaining healthier soil. More carbon is stored by land that is managed this way, and the food that is farmed from it is made more "cool."

Patagonia isn't alone in developing its own eco label. We found a lot of different eco labels that companies use to show their environmental credentials. A bit of research uncovered nearly five hundred different eco labels that can be found on food, beverages, cosmetics, household appliances, furniture, and more. Some of these labels listed carbon emissions per use and per item and estimated carbon emission amounts related to premanufacturing, production, distribution, and end-of-life, or waste, pollution. Others

Top Agricultural Carbon Emitting Countries

1. China
2. India
3. Brazil
4. United States

These four countries alone are responsible for more than one-third of all global greenhouse gas emissions attributable to agricultural production.

"I went overseas looking for the butterfly effect of food. And I found it.

"In my book *You Are Here*, I explained how our everyday actions affect people, places, and things all around the world, and how people, places, and things all around the world affect us at home. Food being one of those things, I roamed to find where our human foodprint meets our human footprint. And it's blatantly obvious: Les Halles, the original site of the Rungis International Market, the world's biggest.

"Les Halles was for centuries the center of the food scene in Paris—the gastronomic capital of the world. It's just off the Seine, a light stroll to the Louvre Museum or Pont Neuf, where the cathedral of Notre Dame rises high in the distance. The neighborhood's quaint stone buildings with wrought iron details in the quintessential Haussmann style of architecture and narrow streets that charm your eyes before the bistros and cafés arrest the rest of senses now lead to a stark, modern shopping mall. The boulangeries and merchant stalls of Les Halles have been replaced by Starbucks, KFC, McDonald's, and Panera Bread—the prongs of our American fast-food diets and reach. And the opposite? Climate change is poised to make extinct wine, coffee, chocolate, and other foods that we love—the hallmarks of French cuisine.

"Broadening our demand beyond fast food and increasing our appetites for the foods Europe has on offer (cheeses, olive oils, and different kinds of fruits and vegetables) might just keep more landmarks intact and our appreciation of culture and history alive.

"It's worth visiting the origins of your favorite meals for education, awareness, and for a taste of what you might be missing."

264

were clearly for marketing purposes, claiming "100% Natural" designations or other factors that aren't particularly meaningful.

Labeling where food comes from and how it's produced, we realize, is a daunting task. According to the research, approximately four billion tons of food are produced annually. Tracing all these foods back to their sources and labeling them is a hard job on its own, never mind the how of it all.

But one of the more insightful details about the carbon emissions of a product is where it comes from because, we learned, small farms in developing countries can have smaller carbon footprints than big industrial farms in the developed world. If these facts were also put on display in the details of a label, we could become better informed about where and how our food is made. This kind of transparency is sorely lacking.

There are five hundred million small-scale farms around the world, with many of their owners uneducated about how food systems can be changed for the better. Which also hampers climate mitigation efforts as well as the effort to bring more climate-friendly foods to market. If the only farms that can afford to live up to international standards and include carbon emissions facts for their products are large-scale farmers, small-scale farmers get shut out of global markets. To be sure, these farms can serve local markets, but it stops them from gaining access to bigger sales opportunities around the world. That's why education and inclusion are so important.

Organizations, like the Global Alliance for the Future of Food, which represent the interests of small farmers, say that the voice of small farms is often left out of international climate talks and negotiations. The most well-known of these discussions are held by the United Nations. Small-farm advocates say that climate agreements could likely benefit from more voices of those on

the ground who have to deal with the ramifications of climate change on a day-to-day basis—like small farmers. At the same time, these farmers could benefit from more resources the United Nations could provide in the form of education assistance.

Until we have labels that are standardized and indicate and define "small-farm produced," we're left to choose by a food's origins.

International markets can also be used as models for us here in the United States. Many countries, we learned, produce and consume far less processed foods than we do, lessening their carbon footprints on the planet. Europe, for example, has the second-largest number of organic farms behind Australia/Oceania. That gives Europeans a far better chance of eating locally grown, organic foods at home than nearly anywhere else on earth. It's likely the reason why organic sales are growing the fastest there, nearly catching up with the United States in sales. As a percentage of diets, statistics show that could be awesome: Europe's population is about twice that of the US.

By changing certain farming methods and by us choosing more plant-based food options over meats and other carbon-intensive foods, the World Resources Institute, which is where we got this data, says we could reduce our global agricultural footprint by as much as 40 percent by 2050. And some research suggests that if all the farms in the world adopted better management practices and took into account climate change in their growing methods (a.k.a. regenerative farming), 100 percent of the world's carbon emissions could be recaptured in a year. Even if that statement is overly optimistic (which other research suggests that it is), we can still do our part by eating cool food.

Carbon labeling can help us make our food decisions based on a more planet-friendly diet. And certainly, it could help us become more aware of which countries are feeding us more

than others and whether their carbon footprints are better. That would be powerful information for us all. The way to harness all that data is through technology and digitalization. Which is one of the reasons why we're devoting our next chapter to the virtual world of food markets and future foods that are grown with the planet in mind and that are different from anything in the history of agriculture.

What You Can Do Today

- Look for carbon labels on products. Note the CO_2e designation—it shows the carbon dioxide energy equivalent; less is best.

- Check where a product comes from by its country of origin label (COOL), and if possible, purchase food from countries that have lower carbon emissions per capita.

- Buy products from small-scale farms when possible.

- Opt for fair-trade foods.

- Ensure labels and certifications are meaningful. "Made from natural ingredients" and "eco friendly" aren't necessarily better for the planet.

- Be on the lookout for foods that come from farms that practice regenerative agriculture; new labels are specifying this.

- Give food companies feedback on products you prefer.

- Contact your public representatives and express your opinion about the World Trade Organization.

Recipe courtesy of *Knorr Future 50 Foods Cookbook*

Moroccan Okra Stew with Sweet Potatoes

INGREDIENTS

¾ lb. *SWEET POTATO*, peeled and cut into cubes

2 small *RED ONIONS*, chopped finely

2 cloves of *GARLIC*, smashed

1 lb. *OKRA*, washed and halved, with the stems removed

1 (14-oz.) *CAN DICED TOMATOES* or 1¼ lbs. fresh tomatoes, roughly chopped

juice of 1 *LEMON*

2 tsp. vegetarian Better Than Bouillon *STOCK CONCENTRATE*

2 tsp. *RAS EL HANOUT* spice mix (can be bought at organic supermarkets or online)

1 bunch *ITALIAN PARSLEY*

METHOD

1 Place the sweet potatoes in a pot with 2¼ cups water; bring to a boil and cook until soft, about 25 minutes. In the meantime, in another pot, heat the oil* and sauté the onion and garlic until slightly browned.

2 Add the okra and stir-fry for 10 minutes. Add the tomatoes and lemon juice, stock concentrate, and ras el hanout. Cover with a lid and let the ingredients simmer for 20 minutes. Add water if necessary (depends on the quality of tomato).

3 Garnish with Italian parsley and serve with brown rice or pita bread.

*for best results add 1–2 tbsp vegetable oil

Aromatic Vietnamese Tofu Pho

INGREDIENTS

9 dried *SHIITAKE MUSHROOMS*

½ lb. *SHALLOTS*, thinly sliced

5 *GARLIC* cloves, peeled and finely sliced

1-inch piece fresh *GINGER*, thinly sliced

3 tbsp. *LIGHT SOY SAUCE*
2½ tbsp. *RICE VINEGAR*
4 pieces *STAR ANISE*

4 *CINNAMON STICKS*
½ bunch of *THAI BASIL*, stems and leaves
½ bunch of *CILANTRO*, stems and leaves
1½ tbsp. Better Than Bouillon *VEGETABLE STOCK CONCENTRATE*

7 oz. *FIRM TOFU*

2 tbsp. *OIL*

7 oz. *FLAT RICE NOODLES*

3 oz. *GREEN BEANS*
3 oz. *CARROTS*
3 oz. *GAI LAN* (Chinese broccoli)
7 large *SHIITAKE MUSHROOMS*, chopped
3 oz. *MUNG BEAN SPROUTS*
8 oz. canned *EDAMAME BEANS*, drained (Geisha makes these)
1 tbsp. of chopped *CILANTRO*
1 tbsp. of *THAI BASIL LEAVES*
4 *LIME* wedges
2 *GREEN ONIONS*, finely chopped

METHOD

1 To prepare the broth, fill a large soup pot with 8½ cups water and add the first 11 ingredients. Bring to a boil, then reduce the heat, and simmer mostly covered for 1½ hours.

2 In a frying pan, fry the tofu over medium heat in 2 tablespoons oil for 3 minutes on each side. Remove from the heat and let cool for 5 minutes, then cut into slices.

3 Boil the rice noodles in a pot for 2–3 minutes, drain and rinse with cold water, and set aside.

4 Cut the green beans, carrots, and gai lan into even shapes and blanch them in boiling water.

5 Heat up a wok with a splash of oil.

6 Stir-fry the mushrooms for 2–3 minutes, then add the blanched vegetables and the beansprouts and edamame beans. Stir-fry for another 3 minutes.

7 Place the vegetables, noodles, and tofu into bowls.

8 Gently pour the remaining broth into the bowls (until everything is just submerged) and finish off with the chopped herbs, lime, and green onion.

VIRTUAL MARKETS

Eat the future, even if it's made out of thin air.

We've become big fans of virtual food markets. A full smorgasbord of cool foods can be found there—without the hindrance of go-betweens or other barriers that we've mentioned in this book, which keep more climate-friendly food products from our local store shelves. Special interests (by that, we mean legacy food groups from industries looking to hang on to their grip on our diets), political interests (like policies that disallow alternative foods from becoming more widely available), financial interests (buyers seeking the lowest costs at the expense of quality), and geographical distances can all be leaped over by going online and picking and choosing your preferred list of climate-friendly foods.

In fact, virtual markets opened up a whole new food world for us because they allowed us to order some of the harder-to-find cool foods that we've pointed out in these pages. Take seaweed. Not at your local supermarket yet?

FAST FACT: Artificial intelligence is affecting the types and amount of food that appear on shelves. Many stores use AI to analyze shopping data and to better predict demand for certain items. It can even help reduce waste by refining shipment orders and monitoring spoilage.

Grocery Pooling

Similar to carpooling, grocery pooling is when you time your food delivery with your neighbors' deliveries so a driver can service more than one household in a trip. Rideshare apps allow this function for basic transportation. Grocery delivery services can, too— there are apps available. By teaming with our neighbors on the same block and ordering group grocery deliveries, we could save half the greenhouse gas emissions that we cause by grocery shopping commutes.

Point and click to order some. Same thing to get "raw" cashews from a family farm or have jackfruit delivered to your door.

Seeking out specific foods was just the beginning of the power we found virtual markets to hold for growers and buyers alike. Actual markets (farmers, co-ops, etc.) are more easily found online. And a particular boon that virtual shopping can bring about is sharing. Virtual markets can bring communities closer together and also provide benefits. Community gardens are used to members sharing the foods they grow with one another. Virtual markets can amp this. Online, neighbors can team up for food deliveries or learn about deals from local farms. Food donations become easier, too: you can request pickups and drop-offs.

Additionally, the virtual world of food shopping can bring with it a peek into the future. Self-described "future food" web shops sell novel foods such as edible insects, microbe-fermented products, and all-in-one superfood meals.

But let's not get ahead of ourselves.

The number one reason for food shopping online is efficiency. According to the USDA, 88 percent of us drive an average of four miles to the grocery store. Just one trip per week from all of us—and we know that we usually make more than one weekly trip—adds up to an insane number of miles: as much as driving to Pluto ten times over the course of a year, according to the math. Hence the reason why we ought to consider virtual shopping with delivery. We learned that it could prove enormously impactful and more climate friendly than all those trips to the store.

The good news is that more of us are, in fact, buying food online—45 percent more, according to the surveys. To be sure, the pandemic supercharged this online movement, but it has been brewing for more than twenty years, we learned, since HomeGrocer.com joined the chorus of internet start-ups in the heady days of the 1990s dot-com craze that had nearly every entrepreneur seeking any product that could be sold

THE COOL WAY TO GET DELIVERY

How you get your food delivered matters. By choosing a longer delivery window, you give drivers more opportunity to batch orders. That saves on the carbon emissions produced by the trucks dropping off your goods. You may even get a discount. And by ordering more food at one time—rather than several small orders—you help avoid emissions, too.

online as a start-up business. Online food sales have steadily ticked up since. And COVID-19 has made them commonplace. In the first few weeks of the pandemic, online food sales soared 300 percent. Our own experiences jibe with that finding. Indeed, how many of us opened an Instacart account or scoured Amazon for groceries for the first time during lockdown? Now one

in four of us Americans keeps shopping that way. Small farmers, mom-and-pop businesses, and those who have developed carbon-friendly foods are seeking support online, too. Which is how the virtual world can help keep the real world cool.

Take Farmbox Direct. It's an online delivery service we learned about that operates throughout the United States and provides fresh fruit and vegetables that are curated to your liking: only organic foods, juicing foods, or diabetic-friendly boxes. The company has direct relationships with farms and produce vendors and ships a custom box to you. The idea is to bring the farmers' market experience to your doorstep.

Then there are the virtual farmers' markets we discussed in our farm-to-table chapter. Many of these are a simple

Google search away. The corporate version of these online grocers is the web stores operated by your favorite supermarkets if they offer that.

The pandemic also accelerated the demand for home-delivered meal kits.

"Most of the developed world discovered meal kits during the pandemic," said Jeff Yorzyk, the director of sustainability for HelloFresh US, from his office in Boulder, Colorado. HelloFresh is the largest meal-kit provider in the country. Its mission is to change the way people eat forever. With millions of meals served around the world, HelloFresh's footprint matters. And it sees its role in the future of food as a critical one.

"The Michigan study really was a stake in the ground," Yorzyk said, referring to a 2019 University of Michigan study that showed the carbon footprint of meal kits is much lower than buying similar ingredients from a grocery store. "It's twenty-five to thirty percent lower carbon footprint per meal served.

> **FAST FACT:**
> HelloFresh's Green Chef is a USDA certified organic company.

And that has to do a bit with supply chain efficiency, logistics efficiency, and then of course the food waste reductions because all of those subtract from a carbon footprint through rotting food waste in a landfill. It just creates less carbon impact on the world."

With the number of meal kits served doubling during the pandemic and meal delivery becoming mainstream, a significant opportunity arose for HelloFresh to hammer home sustainable messaging. "We brought on a partner who can do ingredient-level carbon footprinting. It means that essentially we can start to add up what our recipes look like. In Germany, we launched a pilot in Q4 of 2021 to do on-menu carbon labeling, and it was called Climate Hero, where the lowest carbon recipes on the menu got this little tag that said Climate Hero. It was so popular we never stopped," Yorzyk said. But the messaging has to be sustainable and global.

It works the other way, too. "We basically just keep playing to what our customers are asking for. And then we try to reinforce their decisions as we go forward. Frankly, the more we hear something, like the more customers who are singing the same song, the more that starts to register with us. We use different tools for that, but there's certainly text recognition tools and things that run through our social media to tell us how many times we're seeing certain mentions of things like climate. Same thing with customer emails. So, feedback is super important," Yorzyk said.

Feedback is also the reason why plant-based options are growing.

"Now we're starting to see plant-based 2.0 or maybe even 3.0. We're starting to see some really clean label, simple plant-based foods coming to the market. A lot of them are mushroom or mycelium based. But they've got great nutritional value, and they're cleaner than what we saw previously. As far as I can see, there's sort of this plant-based protein category emerging where they're not trying to be like a burger anymore.

They're a plant-based protein, which is a much better way, I think, of categorizing. We're never going to beat that chargrilled hamburger somebody had at their grandfather's house when they were six years old. So why even try? Let's define it as a separate category," he said.

▲ ▲ ▲ ▲ ▲ ▲ ▲ ▲ ▲

Our online food buying options are clearly expanding. We found lots of big grocery stores and online shopping hubs, such as Mercato, that allow you to choose products from various locations.

And virtual farmers' markets can help us gain direct connections with local growers who may have more cool food to offer than big chain sellers. The opportunity for change is big. That said, some farmers don't have the knowledge (neither would we) to launch their businesses online. That's why nonprofits, government agencies, and food hubs are trying to help with everything from back-office administration to promotion and e-commerce sales platforms. We found apps like GrazeCart, FarmDrop, Farmigo, and GrownBy that are connecting growers to a bigger audience of buyers. And Community Supported Agriculture (CSA) is facilitating more of these relationships online. CSA is a way to buy "shares" in local farms. In return for your shares, members usually get boxes of produce delivered by the participating farms they support. You can check it out at LocalHarvest.org.

Shopping online translates into something else besides getting your groceries delivered conveniently—it produces data. And that data can, in turn, result in efficiencies that lessen the need for us to get into our cars and go. For instance, we learned about appliances that can automatically notify you when you're running out of something. Certain smart refrigerators have built-in sensors that can scan expiration dates. And newer models can, through the

power of artificial intelligence, predict when and what you might want to order from the store. The smart refrigerator then places a delivery order on your behalf. *Knock knock*, and you have your milk before you even knew that you were running out of it.

Smart data usage can lead us toward better decision making. Which is why data is important even if we are talking about something as analog as a tree nut. Couple your smartwatch with data on the availability of healthy, cool foods in your area, and not only could you track your health and wellness, but you could also track the health and wellness of the planet via your own personal carbon emissions calculations.

Imagine your smart device indicating that you should do a better job at heart health. In addition to exercise, foods like tree nuts are good for your heart. With a simple understanding of any nut allergies you might have, the device could alert you about how many nuts you should be eating—and where

SMARTWATCH SMART

Smartwatches are a major tool in helping us realize what it takes for us to get in shape. We track our steps and our heart and lung health. Technology companies are even working on functionalities that can warn of health problems by the sound of your voice. As we know, diet and exercise go hand in hand. The next step in providing health guidance—beyond, say, achieving ten thousand steps a day—is going to be dietary recommendations, according to the experts.

to get them or have them delivered. And beyond being good for your health, we now know that tree nuts are largely good for the environment. So their carbon-saving totals could be displayed. Your carbon footprint then could be helped along with every step you are advised to take. That matters because the

"I really wanted to speak to future foods, something my little organization FootPrint Coalition is actively researching and investing in. A few of the companies we support are MyForest Foods, which replaces livestock farming with planet-friendly meat alternatives grown through natural processes; Nobell, which has developed a technology that uses soybeans to make casein, the protein that makes cheese cheesy; Wildtype is a company that makes delicious filets of fish from cells harvested in petri dishes; Ynsect is pioneering the large-scale production of mealworm protein (and it's good—Stephen Colbert and I ate it on live television); and Zero Acre Farms makes cooking oils that are much better for the planet. To me, the idea of merging technology and innovation with food is the combo we need to arm the world with the power to overcome the ever-growing challenges of climate change."

less pollution in the air, the better off your lungs (and heart), and the more temperate the climate, the less stress over extreme conditions. (Mental health and physical health are increasingly being linked to climate change.)

Many smartwatch apps now include shopping lists, so what we're going on about here isn't so far out there. But for data to help feed us properly and not starve the planet of its natural resources, we have to feed data itself with information. This is controversial, we know. Not everyone wants their likes and dislikes shared with companies that can use that personal information for profit or other purposes. Still, considering that billions of people share their thoughts, hopes, dreams, and desires on social media, an online shopping list may not be too much to ask for.

Vertical Farms

Vertical farms are indoor farms where plants are stacked in rows of containers. The boxed, crop-row-like layers rise vertically, hence the name. Artificial lighting (often powered by alternative energy) and controlled feeding systems and temperatures allow conditions to be acutely monitored and managed, usually by computer sensors. The farms look like huge warehouses with shelving that, instead of products, holds plants.

As much as we pooh-pooh processed foods, the social impetus for them, we learned, was to feed a growing population: the baby boomer generation, or those born between 1946 and 1964. Processed foods can largely be traced to the beginning of this era when that soaring, or booming, population met microwaves,

Get Your Own LED Garden

LED gardens are indoor "gardens" that allow you to grow edible plants, such as leafy vegetables or herbs, on your countertop. They typically come fully equipped with plant boxes and artificial lighting. Most even come with growth kits to help you learn how to tend the mini garden and get the most food out of it.

and chemical advancements gave us ready-made TV dinners. Quantity and convenience were apparently the thing at the time. In any case, health wasn't so much on the consciousness of this revolution—efficiency and quantity often came at the sacrifice of quality. TV dinners, after all, aren't exactly known for their health benefits.

Now, again, we're seeing a world whose population is exploding—headed toward almost ten billion by 2050, according to the data, up from around eight billion as we write—coupled with dire agricultural conditions caused by climate change and fewer natural resources to grow enough food in old, traditional ways.

So, how our food is grown is rising in prominence. And we're not talking about where it's grown or the type of farm (organic or otherwise) as we have in other chapters. We're talking about radical new advancements in technology that allow us to grow food like it's never been grown before.

FOOD FROM AIR?

One of the most intriguing newfangled foods came out of space exploration. During the 1960s, when NASA, the space agency, was attempting to put humans on the moon and further explore deep space, they faced a food challenge: how to feed astronauts for an extended period of time with limited space for storage and limited resources.

That's when they discovered a tiny, single-cell organism, or microbe, that could do what plants naturally do and convert carbon dioxide into food. NASA found that the CO_2 the astronauts exhaled (we all breathe out CO_2) could be captured and converted into nutrients, or the foundation for what we call food. The protein-rich nutrients were then fermented and became edible in different forms. The process is apparently similar to making yogurt. The scientists also learned something else important: the process was sustainable, an endless cycle even, for as long as the astronauts exhaled CO_2, which is to say as long as they lived.

Numerous companies have developed variations of developing food from microbes. It still takes energy and water and tending to, much like growing food in the ground, but it's obviously less resource-intense than raising, say, a cow (not particularly tenable on a spaceship) or sowing seeds. The amount of water needed is small, and

CONTINUED ⟶

the energy used is typically from fossil-free producers, such as wind or solar.

Food from the air will likely be on shelves soon in the form of protein powders or other variations that will supplement common foods. Think pasta, bread, or smoothies. And there are also plans for such future foods to feed other animals besides us: livestock could benefit. That means our food system and the means of agriculture on which we've relied since the dawn of our human history may be about to change, fanning the flame of a new food future.

David Chang, the famed chef, is championing new methods of vertical farming and using the produce from vertical farms in his restaurants. Chang is an owner of AeroFarms, the largest vertical farm in the world, in Jersey City, New Jersey. (IKEA and others are also owners, according to the company.) The indoor farm says on its website that it grows leafy greens in a controlled environment without the need for soil. That's important because the farm says that it uses 95 percent less water than a traditional farm and can grow crops in half the time of outside field methods. Moreover, it says that food can be grown year-round without consideration for adverse climate conditions outdoors. Diseases and pests are also thwarted. We learned that you can actually do a mini version of this yourself at home with hydroponic LED gardens.

These are relatively basic technologies compared to what we discovered being developed in the scientific community—advances such as growing food from thin air or from the pollution we've put into the air. These are future foods like solar proteins, made from pure air and electricity; food made out of the carbon dioxide captured in the atmosphere; 3D-printed food; laboratory-grown meat; algae products; aeroponic-grown plants; hydroponic-grown and cell-based seafood; among other food products and processes designed from sources that we are unaccustomed to associating with farming and agriculture. We use the word *designed* because these aren't foods grown in traditional ways; the means is artificially engineered by humans, much like processed foods but with a different twist of social conscience.

Dr. Pasi Vainikka is the CEO of Solar Foods, a company in Helsinki, Finland, that uses advanced technologies to grow food out of thin air. Its main food product is Solein.

"This is a completely new species," he said when we spoke with him just

Solar Protein

What's a solar protein? It's a new way of growing mass amounts of food by using one of the billions of microbes found in nature and fermenting it. A microbe is a microscopic organism too small to be seen by the naked eye. Microbes come in different forms, including bacteria and fungi, as well as teeny, tiny animals. The bioprocess of growing them into food only needs air and solar energy. The process is twenty times more efficient than photosynthesis, or how typical plants grow, and two hundred times more efficient than growing meat.

before the massive Slush technology conference that takes place every year in Helsinki. (It's called that because it occurs at the end of November, when the temperature hasn't dipped enough to pack snow, leaving it wet—hence, slush.)

Solar Foods didn't begin with the idea to disrupt the food or agriculture industries. But when Solein hits the market, it will be a completely new way of growing food; nothing like it has ever been done in human history.

Solein is not a plant or an animal. It is a single-cell protein that humans can eat, or it can be fed to other animals— livestock. The protein is made by utilizing solar or other renewable electricity to split water (H_2O) into its components: hydrogen and oxygen. Carbon dioxide captured from the air is then mixed with the hydrogen cells along with mineral nutrients. A new organism, Solein, is born, producing its own amino acids, carbohydrates, fats, and vitamins. After it's dried, a fine protein powder is formed.

Vainikka said that alternative energy was the primary driver of the process, not creating a new food type.

"Ten years ago, we started to think, 'What would be the most high-value, high-impact product you could make with solar electricity?'" he recalled.

Electric vehicles had already begun to take off. Solar electricity as a utility had also been exploited. Yet the next huge global sector, besides energy itself, hadn't been explored through the lens of solar: food. And that's because few people understood that solar energy could be used to hack how the earth traditionally produces proteins (growing or breeding them).

"That's when we met our CTO

FAST FACT:
It takes only a small amount of water from the air to grow a full kilogram of Solein. It's being called the most sustainable protein process in the world.

[chief technology officer], who has a bioprocessing background. And he was aware that there are such forms of life that you can actually grow by using electricity directly or indirectly. Indirectly means that we are producing hydrogen gas from air. And that's where the electrical energy is charged in chemical form. Then you feed this gas to organisms that use it instead of sunlight. And that's basically when there is disconnection from agriculture," Vainikka said. In other words, Solar Foods recreated photosynthesis, or what plants do to grow and thrive.

"When you bypass the need for land, all the environmental benefits land on your lap," he said. No habitat loss. No animal slaughter. No pesticide use. No extinction of species or loss of water or other natural resources. And a sustainable, infinitely replaceable source of protein to be had.

As pie-in-the-sky as that may sound, Solein is expected, pending regulatory approval, to be available in grocery stores, well, by the time you're reading these words.

Solein is much like soy or flour or any other protein powder. "It is kind of similar to wheat flour in the sense that you never eat the powder as such, but it can be made into different kinds of foods," Vainikka said. And while "farming the air" could in theory replace the food system as we know it, he believes that Solein will be used more as a companion product at first, reducing the need for animal and vegetable food supplies. Those foods will eventually exist, he believes, as side courses or specialty items.

Take lasagna, for example. Vainikka said you could have Solein as a filler for the pasta, or the meat, or the sauce, reducing the need for one versus the other. Culturally, he said, you might still want to serve lasagna as a meal, just as you might want to serve turkey at Thanksgiving or other foods at culturally or religiously significant times. But the necessity and frequency needs are taken away. "The meat from animals can coexist, but maybe you don't have to have that at every meal every day; it's saved for certain purposes. And then you could also maybe afford to pay a significantly higher price for it, which might be fair for the current form of agriculture. Farmers are continuously suffering from profitability problems. Farming is not really a profitable business, and therefore you need subsidies. So, this coexistence is quite interesting," he said.

Indeed, a new climate-friendly protein that replaces the ways traditional foods are grown or raised and frees up farmers to charge equitably not only creates a new food system but also creates a new food economy.

"It would be kind of a silver bullet, what we're doing; it kind of works," Vainikka said.

We may not be able to order a solar protein burger and CO_2 fries just yet. But we can access food now in ways that were impossible not so long ago—we can quickly find and order a box of fresh tomatoes online, picked from the vine at Harry's farm a couple of towns over, and have it dropped at our front door within a few hours.

There is a fantastic world of food innovation on the horizon—cell-based, solar-based, and carbon-based foods, along with aeroponics and hydroponics—and each advancement is aimed at recasting our agriculture system to something more sustainable, something cooler. By redirecting, for example, the artificial amounts of carbon dioxide that we plume into the atmosphere and storing it in the ground or using it as fertilizer for hothouse gardens, we can feed our starved food supply and cool the planet. And by consuming more of the food that stores more of that carbon—cool foods—we can keep our carbon footprints buried much longer. Like the carbon cycle system itself, this takes things full circle, back into the ground. It also seemed like a good place for us to end this book.

What You Can Do Today

- Order groceries online and save the carbon emissions from driving to the store.

- Choose longer delivery windows so drivers can batch orders.

- Pool grocery deliveries with your neighbors (there are apps for this).

- Shop at virtual farmers' markets to get access to more locally grown and fresh foods.

- Look for apps that connect you directly to local farms.

- Support Community Supported Agriculture that gives you shares in a farm.

- Put your grocery shopping list on your smart device and allow auto ordering and auto refills.

- Look for foods grown in vertical farms (food packages often advertise this).

- Try an LED garden at home to grow your own food indoors.

- Keep an eye out for future foods—they just might save the world.

Recipe courtesy of HelloFresh

Edamame and Cauliflower Fritters

INGREDIENTS

 8 oz. *BROCCOLI*

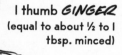 1 clove *GARLIC*

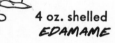 1 thumb *GINGER*
(equal to about ½ to 1 tbsp. minced)

 2 *SCALLIONS*

 4 oz. shelled *EDAMAME*

6 oz. *CAULIFLOWER RICE*

 ¾ c. *TEMPURA BATTER MIX*
(such as Kikkoman)

1 tsp. *COOKING OIL*

3 c. shredded *RED CABBAGE*

 3 tbsp. *SESAME DRESSING*

2 tbsp. *SWEET THAI CHILI SAUCE*, divided

2 tbsp. *MAYONNAISE*

METHOD

1 Adjust rack to top position and preheat oven to 425°F. Wash and dry produce (except cauliflower rice).

2 Cut broccoli florets into bite-size pieces if necessary. Peel and mince or grate garlic and ginger. Trim and thinly slice scallions, separating whites from greens; mince whites.

3 Toss broccoli on a baking sheet with a drizzle of oil, salt, and pepper.

4 Roast on top rack until browned and tender, 15–20 minutes.

291

5 Meanwhile, place edamame, garlic, and ginger in a medium microwave-safe bowl; microwave for 1 minute.

6 Mash half the edamame lightly with a fork. Add cauliflower rice and scallion whites; stir to combine.

7 Stir in tempura mix, ⅓ cup cold water, ½ teaspoon salt, and pepper. (Tip: Batter should be very thick but not dry; add a splash of water if necessary.)

8 Heat a ⅓-inch layer of oil in a large pan over medium-high heat. Once oil is shimmering and hot enough that a drop of batter sizzles when added to the pan, carefully add 1½ tablespoon scoops of batter to pan; press down lightly with a spoon. (Tip: Depending on the size of your pan, you may need to work in batches.) Cook until golden brown and crisp, 3–4 minutes per side. (Tip: If necessary, heat more oil in pan between batches.)

9 Transfer fritters to a paper-towel-lined plate. Season with salt.

10 In a large bowl, toss together roasted broccoli, cabbage, sesame dressing, and half the chili sauce. Season with a pinch of salt and pepper.

11 In a small bowl, whisk together mayonnaise and remaining chili sauce. Add water, one teaspoon at a time, until mixture reaches a drizzling consistency.

12 Divide slaw and fritters between plates. Drizzle chili mayo over fritters. Garnish with scallion greens and serve.

Recipe courtesy of HelloFresh

Crunchy Curried Chickpea Bowls

INGREDIENTS

1 (16-oz.) can **CHICKPEAS**, drained

4 tsp. **OLIVE OIL**

3 oz. **CARROT**

1 **LEMON**

4 oz. **KALE**

¼ c. **GOLDEN RAISINS**

1 tbsp. **CURRY POWDER**, divided

3 tbsp. **BUTTER**

 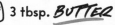
½ c. **BASMATI RICE**

2 tsp. **VEGETABLE STOCK CONCENTRATE**

1 tsp. **SUGAR**

3 c. shredded **RED CABBAGE**

6 tbsp. **SOUR CREAM**

METHOD

1 Adjust rack to top position and preheat oven to 425°F. Wash and dry produce.

2 Drain and rinse chickpeas; thoroughly pat dry with paper towels. Trim, peel, and quarter carrot lengthwise; cut crosswise into ¼-inch-thick pieces. Zest and quarter lemon. Remove and discard any large stems from kale; finely chop leaves. Place raisins in a small bowl with enough hot water just to cover.

3 Toss chickpeas on a baking sheet with a large drizzle of olive oil, half the curry powder (you'll use more in the next step), salt, and pepper. Roast on top rack until crispy, 18–20 minutes. (It's natural for chickpeas to pop a bit as they roast.)

4 While chickpeas roast, melt 1 tablespoon butter in a small pot over high heat. Add carrot and ¼ teaspoon curry powder, (you'll use the rest of the curry powder in step 7). Cook, stirring, until fragrant, 1–2 minutes.

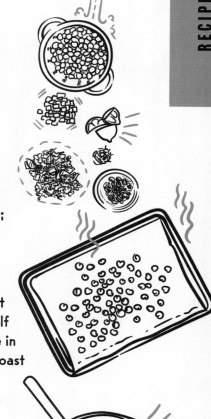

5 Add rice, I cup water, stock concentrate, and a big pinch of salt. Bring to a boil, then cover and reduce to a low simmer. Cook until rice is tender, 15–18 minutes. Keep covered off heat until ready to serve.

6 Meanwhile, in a medium microwave-safe bowl, combine I teaspoon sugar and juice from three lemon wedges; stir to dissolve. Add cabbage and 2 tablespoons water, and season with salt and pepper. Microwave for I minute. Set aside, tossing occasionally, until ready to serve.

7 In a second small bowl, combine sour cream, lemon zest, remaining curry powder, and juice from remaining lemon. Season with salt and pepper. Add water one teaspoon at a time until mixture reaches a drizzling consistency.

8 Heat a large drizzle of olive oil in a large pan over medium-high heat. Add kale and season with salt and pepper. Cook, stirring occasionally, until tender, 5–7 minutes.

9 Stir in I tablespoon butter until melted. Remove from heat.

10 Fluff rice with a fork; stir in I tablespoon butter and season with salt and pepper.

11 Divide rice between bowls. Top with kale, pickled cabbage (draining first), and chickpeas in separate sections. Drain and sprinkle raisins (roughly chopping first if desired) over top. Drizzle with dressing and serve.

CONCLUSION

Even though this is a conclusion,
a book like this never really ends.

Cool Food is a dynamic approach to addressing the challenges that climate change presents; it's ever evolving. And sure, it takes a village to foster the kind of change we are talking about. But what if we could begin that change with just one bite, just one action? That was the proposition upon which this book began. And here, as we attempt to answer that, the solution is clear: the opportunity to alter the course of our planet's destructive path toward a more positive future is within our grasp. It's as close to us as our mouths and our stomachs.

To be sure, no one food will fix things. As we learned, so much goes into a single bite of food—where it's grown; how it's transported; whether it's refrigerated; and how much waste is left over; never mind the environmental practices of the market or restaurant from which we purchased that bite—that a single "super cool food"

Check out
CoolFoodBook.com
for special
promotions,
offers, and
more. Or scan
the QR Code
below:

cannot exist. Still, a menu of foods and actions designed to cool the planet can do just that. We're downright thrilled that these menus along with their carbon disclosures are catching on at restaurants and markets the world over, and we hope to see more carbon counts accompanying calorie counts to help us make more-informed decisions. We also hope that we've done our bit to help.

Every chapter in this book has its own list of big takeaways that can facilitate sustainable decision making. We do, though, have our favorites:

1. Eat what's in season.

2. Go for organic.

3. Opt for meal kits to mitigate food waste.

4. Try incorporating more ancient foods into your diet.

5. Look for the carbon label on packaging or menu boards.

Of all the takeaways we just listed, we believe carbon labeling offers the biggest promise for change. Armed with that succinct bit of knowledge, we can make climate-smart choices. And that's what this book is supposed to be about.

Cool Foodprint Calculator

Check out the Foodprint Calculator at
https://MyEmissions.green/Food-Carbon-Footprint-Calculator/
where you can log on, enter a food choice, and find out its CO_2 quotient.

THANKS FROM THE BOTTOM
OF OUR STOMACHS FOR TAKING
THIS JOURNEY WITH US.

EAT COOL.

Recipe Index

The source notes and references for this book
can be found at CoolFoodBook.com.

ACKNOWLEDGMENTS

Like any good meal, this book had a lot of ingredients and involved the hard work of a lot of people. They deserve much more recognition than we can fit on this page. For us to do justice and give individual shout-outs, we'd have to do a whole other book. Instead, we've come up with a list of our special ingredients: Susan Downey, Julia Hodges, Emily Ford, Pierre Moulene, Nate Merritt, Joy Fehily, Anna Bamford, Mel Berger, Susan Raihofer, Margaret Riley, Erin Picone, Maria Toscano, Josh Stanton, Anthony Goff, Rick Bleiweiss, Christina Boys, Stephanie Stanton, Kathryn English, Matthew Marley, Rachel Sanders, Rebecca Malzhan, Isabella Bedoya, Caitlin Vander Meulen, and Josie Woodbridge.

Inside these pages we were fortunate to be introduced to so many insightful individuals: Rachel Stroer, Caroline Sluyter, Luis Acuña, Sam Platt, Mike Graham, Tim Flannery, Linda and Scott Neuman, Dr. Alex McAlvay, Allison Hope, Andy Finton, Alice Waters, Michael Oshman, Douglas McMaster, Dr. Jean Buzby, Kaj Török, Charles Spence, Mayor Eric Adams, Paula Daniels, Richard Waite, Phillip Grant, Gabriela D'Arrigo, Stefanie Katzman, Hanneke Faber, Matthew Isaacs, Jeff Yorzyk, and Dr. Pasi Vainikka. As well as the people who helped connect these voices to us: Tammy Kimbler, Hannah Depin, Reana Kovalcik, Su Taylor, Brianna Hudson, Stevenson Swanson, Alessandra Clark, Jaemie Ballesteros Altman, Rey Day, Anna Lilja, Lovisa Haeger, Erfan Jalilian, Linus Kondén, Rachel Atcheson, Jillian Holzer, Courtney Lambert, and Victoria Musso.

Thank you all. Please take a bow.

50 Future Foods

1. Laver seaweed
2. Wakame seaweed
3. Adzuki beans
4. Black turtle beans
5. Board beans
   (fava beans)
6. Bambara groundnuts/
   beans
7. Cowpeas
8. Lentils
9. Marama beans
10. Mung beans
11. Soy beans
12. Nopales
13. Amaranth
14. Buckwheat
15. Finger millet
16. Fonio
17. Khorasan wheat
18. Quinoa
19. Spelt
20. Teff
21. Wild rice
22. Pumpkin flowers
23. Okra
24. Orange tomatoes
25. Beet greens
26. Broccoli rabe

27. Kale

28. Moringa

29. Pak-choi or bok-choy

30. Pumpkin leaves

31. Red cabbage

32. Spinach

33. Watercress

34. Enoki mushrooms

35. Maitake mushrooms

36. Saffron milk cap mushrooms

37. Flax seeds

38. Hemp seeds

39. Sesame seeds

40. Walnuts

41. Black salsify

42. Parsley root

43. White icicle radish

44. Alfalfa sprouts

45. Sprouted kidney beans

46. Sprouted chickpeas

47. Lotus root

48. Ube (purple yam)

49. Yam bean root

50. Red Indonesian sweet potatoes

A Word about Our Paper Manufacturer

PAPER: A MORE NATURAL, SUSTAINABLE PRODUCT

NORPAC, located in Longview, Washington (330 miles from Blackstone Publishing), recovers and reuses 400,000 tons of mixed paper and corrugated containers annually. Their ongoing $50 million investment in a state-of-the-art recycled fiber plant is expected to double that volume.

NORPAC ensures that when wood chips are used, they originate from certified, responsibly managed, replanted, and renewable forests. The responsibly managed forests providing this wood benefit ecological and environmental health by preventing soil erosion, preserving watersheds and wetlands, and removing CO_2 and other harmful emissions from the atmosphere.

All their fiber, both recycled and wood fiber, may be purchased as chain of custody certified under the following global certification programs: Forest Stewardship Council® (FSC-C132345), Sustainable Forestry Initiative® (SFI-01688), and Programme for the Endorsement of Forest Certification® (PEFC-29-31-404).

To minimize the use of harmful chemicals, NORPAC's high-yield pulping and peroxide bleaching processes are totally chlorine-free (TCF). Both their mechanical and recycled fiber pulping processes are process chlorine-free (PCF), and most of NORPAC's graphic papers are totally chlorine-free (TCF). Papers made with kraft pulp, like Orca uncoated freesheet grades, are elemental chlorine-free (ECF).

At Blackstone, we believe that environmentally sustainable behavior not only benefits our organization but helps contribute to the greater good of our whole planet. We are proud to work in partnership with NORPAC, who has made their community responsibilities central to their business and continually works to be reliable stewards of the environment. We are dedicated to ensuring our efforts contribute to a much cooler future.

Learn more at:
www.NORPACPaper.com/Sustainability-and-Environmental-Responsibility

Not The End

You read the book, now what?

To continue the Cool Food journey, visit the URL or use the QR code below.

CoolFoodBook.com